good food

Anneka Manning was born in Cooma, New South Wales, Australia
in 1970. She has been food editor of *australian good taste*
magazine since its inception in July 1996.

good food
anneka manning

KÖNEMANN

The Text Publishing Company
171 La Trobe Street
Melbourne Victoria 3000
Australia

Designed by Lou Fay

Copyright © 2001 of this edition:
Könemann Verlagsgesellschaft mbH
Bonner Strasse 126, D-50968 Cologne

Production: Ursula Schümer
Printing and Binding: Kossuth Printing House Co., Budapest
Printed in Hungary

ISBN 3-8290-5902-7
10 9 8 7 6 5 4 3 2 1

Some of the material in this book has previously been published in
australian good taste.

contents

foreword
by anneka manning

good food is about cooking with fresh produce at its best, making the most of fruits and vegetables in their natural season, when they're generally at their cheapest. It's about using peaches at their most luscious, corn at its sweetest, asparagus at its most tender and limes at their juiciest.

I grew up on a sheep and cattle property on the New South Wales-Victorian border. On our farm the seasons seemed well defined, not only by shearing or calving times, but by the array of fresh vegetables in Dad's garden. Cabbages and broccoli were picked in autumn and winter, there were beans in late spring and summer, and strawberries in mid-summer.

I now know, however, that identifying the seasons in Australia is a tricky business. We live in a vast country with a huge range of climatic conditions. These conditions vary from state to state and from region to region. This means, for example, that strawberries can be grown in Queensland in July and August and be available in southern states during winter. Providing the supply is bountiful, fresh produce can be enjoyed almost anywhere at any time in Australia.

This ability to distribute and share our produce also means that the seasons are extended. The cherry supply, for instance, starts in

November with produce from the Orange, Young and Batlow areas of New South Wales, the Stoneville, Donnybrook and Manjimup areas of Western Australia and from the Adelaide Hills in South Australia (just to mention a few) reaching the markets nationally. There are later pickings in December, and in January when the Huon and Channel districts in Tasmania start harvesting.

Demand also influences supply. If consumers want a particular fruit or vegetable to be in the shops out of its natural season, such as apples or tomatoes, producers will endeavour to meet this demand. In truth, though, there are very few fruit and vegetable varieties that can be grown, naturally, year-round, despite our varying climatic conditions. Still, this doesn't stop us from trying to breed varieties that will produce a 52-week supply.

Out-of-season fruit and vegetables can sometimes be of poor quality. Eat a sundowner apple (surely one of the most beautiful eating apples) when the variety is not at its peak, say in late spring or early summer, and you will be reluctant to try one again. Pick one up in winter and you'll be a fan forever. And if you compare a floury, flavourless winter tomato to a summer or autumn tomato you will soon learn to stick to the canned variety until winter passes.

Personally, I like the idea of *not* being able to get raspberries or cherries in winter and pears or chestnuts in summer. That, to me, defines a season. It makes you appreciate particular kinds of produce—enjoy them to the full for a finite period, no matter how short. It makes you joyfully anticipate the next season.

But if you really want to eat specific fruits and vegetables all year why not preserve the season instead of chasing it? It makes sense to prepare fresh tomato sauce with the pulpiest, reddest tomatoes you can find, and bottle it. Or to preserve stone fruit, locking in the essence of summer to savour in mid-winter.

While researching this book I talked to many growers, and to the people who work with them to supply the main markets around Australia. They have helped me compile the seasonal produce lists that appear at the beginning of each section. I have endeavoured to include the major varieties of fruit and vegetables available in Australia to indicate when they are at their best, not just when you will find them in store. Asparagus, for example, can be found in stores in autumn, but it is at its peak in spring.

Be mindful that seasonality can depend on the weather. A hot spell or too much rain, for instance, will affect the quantity and quality of fresh produce available. The seasonal produce lists are your guide to buying. Once you start to buy according to the 'natural seasons', your cooking will become so much more enjoyable.

As food editor of *australian good taste* magazine I can vouch for every recipe in *good food*: they are simple, approachable and, above all, absolutely delicious. The ingredients are widely available; the recipes will let you make a big impression with little effort. Fresh produce in simple combinations are used to produce food that is irresistible. These recipes will become familiar, comfort you, make you and others feel good and help you to entertain. You will come back to time and time again, as I have.

One more important point: this is 'no tricks' food. What you see is what you get, and you'll easily achieve the same presentation standard you see on these pages.

I chose these recipes because they *really* work and because I can't get through a season without them. They are the work of *australian good taste* regulars and I recommend them to you wholeheartedly.

I have thrown a few chocolate recipes and other extras in for good measure. Lucky for us, they have no real season and can be enjoyed at any time of the year.

Enjoy *good food!*

Anneka Manning
Food editor, *australian good taste*

spring

a season of growth and new beginnings

When freshly-harvested produce is on hand, cooking is taken to a higher level. The flavours are more intense, the colours more vivid and the textures more true to their variety.

And no food is fresher than the vegetables, herbs or fruit you pick from your *own* garden. There is no better season than spring to get enthused about starting a vegetable patch, filling a few terracotta pots with herbs or planting a citrus tree.

I have only discovered the delights and rewards of gardening in the last few years. We don't have much space, but we do have enough to give us a season of tomatoes, a full supply of herbs year-round, chillies for endless jars of harissa (see p 28) and a few strawberries—most of which get

eaten between the garden and kitchen!

Choose plants that will suit not only the space you have to dedicate to them, but also the climate in which you live. Good vegetables to plant in spring include lettuces (especially oakleaf, mignonette, cos and butter varieties), chillies, beans, tomatoes, capsicum, cucumber (non-trailing types like the 'green apple' variety are good to grow in pots), eggplants and squash.

If you are new to gardening, don't overlook herbs. They are possibly the most useful and easiest plants of all to grow. And all you really need is a pot of well-drained soil and a spot in the sun.

Spring is the best time to sow seeds or plant seedlings of perennials like thyme, marjoram, rosemary, oregano, mint, sage, winter sage, chives, parsley and French sorrel. Spring is also the

time to replant annuals like rocket, chervil, coriander, basil and dill. But make sure you plant your basil last and only when winter is well and truly over.

Just think what your backyard can offer you: handfuls of fresh flavoured whole parsley leaves to throw into a salad; peppery rocket to sprinkle over pizza straight from the oven; basil to toss through pasta and spring vegetables (see p 29); freshly snipped chives to season a Sunday night omelette; pungent coriander to finish off that Thai soup or Middle Eastern-spiced lentils; refreshing, fragrant mint to enhance pineapple granita (see p 53).

Garden fresh is the best guide to the natural seasons of Australian produce. Try it, you'll love it.

spring's best
a guide to help you use produce at the height of its season

vegetables

- artichokes:
  globe (early to mid)
  Jerusalem (early)
- Asian greens:
  bok choy
  choy sum
  gai lum
  Chinese cabbage
  (wong nga bok)
- asparagus
- beans:
  broad (fava or lima) (early)
  green
  Italian flat (late)
- beetroot (beet)
- broccoli
- brussels sprouts (early to mid)
- cabbage
- capsicum (pepper) (mid to late)
- cauliflower
- chillies
- corn (late)
- cucumber (late)
- fennel (early)
- garlic
- ginger (early)
- kohlrabi (early to mid)
- leeks
- lettuce
- mushrooms (cultivated)
- onions:
  brown
  green shallots/green onions/
  scallions
  French shallots/eschallots
  red/Spanish
  spring
  white
- parsnip (early)

- peas:
  green
  snow (early to mid)
  sugar snap
- potatoes (general)
- pumpkin
- radish
- rhubarb
- silverbeet (early to mid)
- spinach/English spinach
  (early to mid)
- swede
- tomatoes (mid to late)
- watercress
- witlof (chicory) (mid to late)
- zucchini (late)

fruit

- apples:
  bonza (early)
  granny smith (early to mid)
  lady william (early to mid)
  red delicious
  sundowner (early to mid)
- avocados
- bananas
- berries:
  boysenberries (late)
  blueberries (late)
  mulberries (late)
  strawberries
  young berries (late)
- cherries (late)
- grapefruit:
  pink (early)
  yellow
- grapes (late)

- lemons (early to mid)
- loquat (rush orange) (late)
- mandarins (early)
- mangoes (mid to late)
- melons:
  honeydew (mid to late)
  rockmelon (cantaloupe)
  (mid to late)
  watermelon (mid to late)
- nectarines (late)
- oranges:
  navel (early to mid)
  blood (early)
  valencia (mid to late)
- papaya (late)
- pawpaw (mid to late)
- peaches (late)
- pineapple (mid to late)

This information may vary slightly depending on where you live and/or weather conditions.

Serve these simple rolls with drinks or take them on picnics.
Lavoche, sometimes spelt lavache, is a Middle Eastern flatbread
that can either be crisp or soft. The soft variety, usually sold in
rectangular pieces, is the one you need for this recipe.

smoked trout
lavoche rolls

makes: 24   prep: 20 mins

3	lavoche bread pieces
75g	(1/2 cup) baby spinach leaves, stalks trimmed
400g	(1 pound) sliced smoked trout

ricotta filling

200g	(1 cup) fresh ricotta
100g	(7 tbs) cream cheese
2 tsp	fresh lemon juice, or to taste
	Salt & ground black pepper, to taste

1 To make the ricotta filling, place the ricotta, cream cheese, lemon juice and salt and pepper to taste in the bowl of a food processor and process until combined. Transfer to a small bowl.

2 Lay lavoche bread pieces flat on a damp, clean tea towel. Spread the ricotta mixture evenly over the lavoche bread. Top with a layer of the spinach leaves and then a layer of smoked trout. Season with pepper. Roll up each lavoche bread piece as tightly as possible. Wrap in plastic wrap and place in the fridge until ready to serve (for up to 12 hours).

3 Cut into 3cm-thick slices to serve.

Many of us have never tasted the earthy sweetness of freshly cooked beetroot (beets) and only remember the canned stuff that made school sandwiches soggy. If you can't find cute-looking baby beetroot, simply use 1 bunch medium-sized beetroot but use more baby spinach instead of beetroot leaves. Cook them whole for about 35 minutes and then peel and quarter them.

asparagus beetroot spinach & walnut salad

serves: 8 as an entree   prep: 25 mins   cooking: 20–25 mins

4	bunches baby beetroot, including leaves
185mls	($^3/_4$ cup) olive oil
160g	(1$^1/_4$ cups) walnuts
4	bunches asparagus, trimmed
240g	(2$^1/_4$ cups) baby spinach, washed, dried
300g	(2$^3/_4$ cups) goat's cheese, cut into 5mm-thick slices

walnut dressing

1$^1/_2$ tbs	balsamic vinegar
	Salt & ground black pepper, to taste

1 Trim the beetroot stalks, leaving about 3cm still attached to the bulbs. Wash 50g ($^1/_4$ cup) of the beetroot leaves, dry and set aside. Reserve remaining leaves for another use.

2 Place the beetroot in a large saucepan, cover with cold water and bring to the boil over high heat. Reduce the heat to medium-high and cook for 15 minutes or until tender when tested with a skewer. Drain and set aside to cool.

3 Heat the olive oil in a frying pan over medium heat. Add the walnuts, reduce heat to medium-low and cook, stirring occasionally, for 10 minutes or until lightly browned. Remove the walnuts from the pan with a slotted spoon and drain on paper towel. Reserve the oil to make the walnut dressing.

4 Bring a large saucepan of water to the boil. Add the asparagus and cook for 2 minutes or until tender crisp. Drain and refresh under cold running water. Drain well.

5 Peel the beetroot. Shred the reserved beetroot leaves. Combine the baby spinach with the beetroot leaves in a bowl.

6 To make the walnut dressing, place balsamic vinegar in a medium bowl and gradually whisk in the reserved walnut oil. Season with salt and pepper.

7 To serve, divide the baby spinach mixture among serving plates. Arrange beetroot, asparagus and goat's cheese on top. Sprinkle with walnuts and drizzle with the walnut dressing.

ASPARAGUS

■ To prepare asparagus for cooking, hold the spears one by one close to the base end and gently bend—they will snap where they naturally need to be trimmed.

■ Steam asparagus until bright green or toss with a little olive oil and cook on a chargrill until tender. Drizzle with extra virgin olive oil and some lemon juice while still warm and sprinkle with plenty of ground black pepper and parmesan shavings.

■ Try throwing a few sprigs of mint into the cooking water when boiling asparagus.

good asparagus partners: eggs, olive oil, butter, cream, leeks, parmesan, balsamic vinegar, hollandaise sauce, mint, black pepper.

Known as the porridge of the gods, a true risotto can only be made using Italian rice varieties that have a great capacity to absorb liquid while releasing surface starch to add to the creaminess of this dish. Arborio—a big, plump, pearl-centred rice—is one and is readily available.

basic herb risotto
with parmesan

serves: 6 as an entree   prep: 10 mins   cooking: 30–35 mins

5¹/₂ cups	vegetable or chicken stock
60mls	(¹/₄ cup) extra virgin olive oil
20g	(1 tbs) butter
1	brown onion, finely chopped
2	garlic cloves, finely chopped
440g	(2 cups) Arborio rice
¹/₃ cup	chopped mixed fresh herbs (like parsley, basil and sage)
40g	(¹/₂ cup) grated parmesan
20g	(1 tbs) butter, extra
	Ground black pepper, to taste

1 Bring the stock just to the boil in a saucepan. Reduce heat and hold the stock at a gentle simmer.

2 Heat the olive oil and butter in a heavy-based saucepan over medium heat. Add the onion and cook, stirring often, for 3 minutes. Add the garlic and cook, stirring, for 2–4 minutes or until the onion is soft but not coloured.

3 Add the Arborio rice and stir over medium heat for 1 minute or until well coated with oil and butter and the grains have become slightly glassy in appearance.

4 Add a ladleful of the simmering stock to the rice and use a wooden spoon to stir constantly over medium heat until the liquid is completely absorbed. Continue to add the stock, a small ladleful (about ¹/₄ cup) at a time, stirring constantly, and allow the liquid to be absorbed before adding the next lot. Cook until the rice is tender yet firm to the bite and the risotto is creamy. Start tasting after about 15 minutes — it will probably take about 20–25 minutes to cook.

5 Remove the risotto from the heat and stir in the chopped herbs, parmesan and extra butter. Season with pepper. Serve immediately.

vegetable lasagne

serves: 6   prep: 20 mins   cooking: 45 mins

300g   (1³/₄ cups) low-fat fresh ricotta
1 tbs   olive tapenade (black olive paste)
4   (200g) fresh lasagne sheets
250mls   (1 cup) basic tomato sauce (p 131)
250g   (¹/₂ small) butternut pumpkin,
    peeled, deseeded, cut into
    thin slices
¹/₄ tsp   ground nutmeg
    Cracked black pepper, to taste
6   small (about 350g) egg
    tomatoes, sliced
1   bunch English spinach,
    washed, stems removed

1 Preheat oven to 200°C. Cover a baking tray with non-stick baking paper.

2 Combine the ricotta and the tapenade in a small mixing bowl with a fork.

3 Place a sheet of pasta on the lined baking tray. Spoon 60mls (¹/₄ cup) tomato sauce over the pasta and spread evenly. Layer half of the pumpkin slices over the sauce. Sprinkle over half of the nutmeg and some pepper. Top with half of the tomato slices and half of the spinach.

4 Top with another sheet of pasta and spread with 60mls (¹/₄ cup) tomato sauce. Spread the ricotta mixture evenly over the top of the sauce.

5 Layer with another sheet of pasta and spread with 60mls (¹/₄ cup) tomato sauce. Layer with the remaining pumpkin slices and sprinkle with the rest of the nutmeg and some pepper. Top with the remaining spinach.

6 Spread the remaining tomato sauce over the spinach and top with a final layer of pasta. Top with the remaining tomato slices.

7 Bake in preheated oven for 45 minutes or until the pumpkin is tender when tested with a skewer. Serve warm.

Risoni, also known as orzo, is a tiny rice-shaped pasta. It is an

excellent substitute for rice and can be used in soups too.

risoni with prawns

serves: 6 as an entree, 4 as a main   prep: 10–15 mins   cooking: 15–20 mins

60mls	(1/4 cup) olive oil
500g	(16 oz) risoni
750g	(1 1/4 pounds) green prawns, peeled with tails left intact, deveined
375mls	(1 1/2 cups) fish or vegetable stock
375mls	(1 1/2 cups) dry white wine
1	lemon
100g	(5 tbs) butter, cubed
1/2 cup	chopped fresh continental parsley
2 tbs	drained capers

1 Bring a large saucepan of water to a rapid boil. Add 1 tsp of the olive oil and then the risoni. Stir to prevent the risoni from sticking to the bottom of the saucepan. Boil for 8 minutes or until al dente. Drain, transfer to a bowl and toss with 3 tsp of the remaining olive oil. Cover to keep warm and set aside.

2 Meanwhile, heat the remaining 2 tbs of olive oil in a large frying pan over high heat. Add the prawns and toss for 2–3 minutes or until prawns change colour and are just cooked. Use a slotted spoon to remove the prawns from the pan and set aside.

3 Add the stock and the white wine to the pan and simmer for 10 minutes or until reduced to 440mls (1 3/4 cups).

4 Meanwhile, peel rind from the lemon using a vegetable peeler. Remove white pith from the rind and cut the rind into thin strips. (Alternatively use a zester.) Squeeze the lemon and reserve juice.

5 Add the butter and parsley to the reduced stock and wine in the pan, and stir over low heat until butter is melted. Remove from heat and add to the risoni with the prawns, lemon rind and juice and capers. Toss to combine. Serve warm or at room temperature.

This updated version of potato salad is substantial enough for a light meal on its own. Try other waxy varieties of potatoes, like pink fir apple, kipfler and pink eye, instead of the desiree. Just keep in mind their size, as this will affect the cooking time.

potato salad with chicken & prosciutto

serves: 6 as a light meal   prep: 10–15 mins   cooking: 20–25 mins

	Olive oil, for greasing chargrill
3	single chicken breast fillets, trimmed
1.5kg	(3 pounds) small desiree potatoes, halved
120g	(1/4 pound) thin prosciutto slices, cut into thin strips
	Chopped fresh chives, to garnish

chive dressing

250mls	(1 cup) sour light cream
1 tbs	wholegrain mustard
1 tbs	fresh lemon juice
2 tsp	white wine vinegar
2 tsp	sugar
60mls	(1/4 cup) light olive oil
1/3 cup	finely chopped fresh chives
	Salt & ground black pepper, to taste

1 Brush chargrill with the olive oil to grease and then preheat over medium heat.

2 Cook the chicken fillets on preheated chargrill for 4–5 minutes each side or until just cooked through. Remove from the chargrill and set aside to cool.

3 Place the potatoes in a large saucepan, cover with cold water and bring to the boil. Boil, partially covered, for 12–15 minutes or until tender. (See microwave tip.) Cut each potato into four wedges.

4 Meanwhile, cook the prosciutto in a non-stick frying pan over medium heat for 3 minutes or until crisp. Drain on paper towel.

5 To make the dressing, place the sour cream, mustard, lemon juice, vinegar and sugar in the bowl of a food processor and process until just combined. With the motor running, gradually add the oil in a thin stream until mixture is evenly combined and thickened. Stir in the chives and season with salt and pepper.

6 Just before serving, thinly slice the cooled chicken fillets across the grain. Layer the chicken slices, potato wedges and dressing in serving bowls. Top with the prosciutto and garnish with the chopped chives.

microwave tip: pierce the potato halves twice with a fork and place around outer edge of turntable. Cook for 7–10 minutes on High/850watts/100% (potatoes should still be firm). Wrap in foil and stand 5 minutes.

These Mediterranean-inspired lamb burgers, and the

variations below, will put the take-away varieties to shame.

Hummus can be used in place of the baba ganoush if you like.

mediterranean lamb burgers on Turkish bread

serves: 6   prep: 20–25 mins (plus 30 mins chilling time)   cooking: 25–30 mins

1¹/₂   red capsicums (peppers),
       quartered, deseeded
2¹/₂ tbs   olive oil
6   pieces Turkish bread,
       split in half
130g   (¹/₂ cup) baba ganoush
1   bunch rocket, trimmed

lamb patties
750g   (1³/₄ pounds) lamb mince
       (preferably from leg trim-
       mings)
1   large brown onion, grated
2   garlic cloves, crushed
2 tsp ground cumin
2 tsp Tabasco sauce (optional),
       or to taste
¹/₄ cup   chopped fresh mint
70g   (1 cup) breadcrumbs,
       made from day-old bread
1   egg, lightly whisked
       Salt & ground black pepper

1 To make the lamb patties, place the lamb mince, onion, garlic, cumin, Tabasco sauce, mint, breadcrumbs and egg in a large bowl. Season with salt and pepper. Mix with your hands until evenly combined.

2 Divide the patty mixture into six equal portions. Use your hands to shape each portion into a patty about 10cm (3.9 in) in diameter and 1.5cm (¹/₃ in) thick. Place the patties onto a tray lined with greaseproof paper. Cover with plastic wrap and place in the fridge for at least 30 minutes to rest.

3 Meanwhile, preheat grill on high. Brush the capsicum quarters with a little of the olive oil and then place them, skin side up, under preheated grill and cook for 5–10 minutes or until charred and blistered. Place the capsicum in a plastic bag, seal and set aside for 10 minutes (this helps lift the skin). Leave the grill on. Peel the skin away from the capsicum and cut each quarter in half. Set aside.

4 Heat half the remaining olive oil in a large, non-stick frying pan over medium-low heat and cook half the lamb patties for about 4 minutes on each side or until browned and cooked through. Transfer the patties to a plate, set aside and keep warm. Repeat with the remaining oil and patties.

5 Meanwhile, place the Turkish bread pieces, cut side up, under preheated grill and toast for 1 minute or until golden.

6 Spread the bottom halves of the toasted Turkish bread with the baba ganoush. Top each with a lamb patty, roasted capsicum and some rocket. Sprinkle with salt and pepper, cover with the remaining Turkish bread halves and serve immediately.

variations

■ **Thai chicken burgers:** replace lamb with chicken mince (preferably thigh fillet mince); replace brown onion with ¹/₂ bunch green shallots, thinly sliced; replace ground cumin and Tabasco sauce with 2 tbs fresh lemon juice, 1 lemon grass stem (pale section only), finely chopped and 1 fresh birdseye chilli, finely chopped; and replace mint with fresh coriander. Increase the breadcrumbs to 105g (1¹/₂ cups). Halve cooked patties and wrap in pitta bread with sweet chilli sauce, cucumber slices and snow pea sprouts.

■ **basic beef burgers:** replace the lamb mince with beef mince (like topside); replace the ground cumin with 1 tbs Worcestershire sauce; and replace the mint with fresh continental parsley. Serve on hamburger buns and top with cheddar cheese, sliced tomato, homemade (see p 68) or bought tomato sauce and shredded iceberg lettuce leaves.

There is no need to complicate things when cooking with asparagus. Simplicity is the key. Even though it may be available at other times during the year you will find asparagus at its best and in abundance in spring. Look for slender, perky stems that have tightly closed heads.

penne with vegetables basil & bacon

serves: 4   prep: 15 mins   cooking: 10 mins

CHILLI

■ Make a fiery harissa paste by processing 100g fresh red chillies (you can remove the seeds if you wish), 6 garlic cloves, 2 tbs coriander seeds, 2 tbs chopped fresh coriander, 2 tsp dried mint, 1¹/₂ tsp caraway seeds, 2 tbs olive oil and a pinch of salt in a food processor until a stiff paste forms. You may need a little more oil. Keep it covered with a thin layer of olive oil in a jar in the fridge. It should keep for up to 3 months. Serve it alongside barbecued lamb and beef, add to Moroccan-spiced lamb casseroles, add a little to tomato sauces or stir some through natural yoghurt and serve with lamb burgers (see p 27)— remember, a little goes a long way.

■ For a Thai green curry paste process 10 fresh green chillies (deseeded if you want), 2 brown onions, 1 bunch fresh coriander, leaves, roots and stems chopped, 4 garlic cloves, 5cm (12 in) piece fresh ginger, peeled and chopped, 2¹/₂ tsp coriander seeds, 1¹/₂ tsp ground cumin, 1 tsp ground turmeric, 1 tsp black peppercorns and 1 tbs peanut oil in a food processor until a smooth paste forms. You may need to add a little more oil. Keep it covered with a thin layer of peanut oil in a clean jar in the fridge for up to 4 months.

good chilli partners: lime, garlic, cumin, fresh and dried coriander, noodles, tomatoes, chicken, seafood, ginger, onion.

500g	(16 oz) dried penne pasta
2¹/₂ tbs	olive oil
3	middle bacon rashers, rind removed, roughly chopped
2	garlic cloves, crushed
1	bunch asparagus, trimmed, cut into 4cm lengths
200g	(³/₄ cup) yellow button squash or zucchini, sliced
	Salt & ground black pepper, to taste
2	medium ripe tomatoes, diced
¹/₃ cup	torn fresh basil leaves

1 Cook the pasta in a large saucepan of salted boiling water, following packet directions, until al dente.

2 Meanwhile, heat 1 tsp of the olive oil in a medium frying pan over medium heat. Add the bacon and cook for 3–4 minutes or until crisp. Remove the bacon from the pan with a slotted spoon and drain on paper towel.

3 Add the remaining olive oil, garlic, asparagus, squash or zucchini and salt and pepper to the frying pan and cook over medium heat, stirring occasionally, for 3 minutes. Stir in the diced tomatoes, cover and cook for 2–3 minutes or until tomatoes are just heated through.

4 Drain the pasta and return it to the saucepan. Stir in the vegetable mixture and bacon and cook over medium heat for 1 minute or until just heated through. Serve immediately.

spiced coconut pilaf with lamb

serves: 4 as a main, 6 as a light meal prep: 15 mins
(plus 3–5 mins standing time) cooking: 35–45 mins

1 tsp **ground cumin**
       Pinch of salt
       Vegetable oil, for greasing
12   **lamb cutlets**
       Lemon wedges, to serve

spiced coconut pilaf

300g **(1 1/2 cups) basmati rice**
2 1/2 tbs **vegetable oil**
70g **(1/2 cup) slivered almonds**
2 **medium brown onions, halved, finely sliced**
2 **garlic cloves, finely chopped**
1 **5cm (12 in) piece fresh ginger, peeled, finely chopped**
1 tsp **ground cinnamon**
1/4 tsp **cardamom seeds**
6 **whole cloves**
1/4 tsp **chilli powder**
500mls **(2 cups) chicken stock**
125mls **(1/2 cup) coconut milk**
       Pinch of salt, or to taste
75g **(1/2 cup) currants**
1/3 cup **roughly chopped fresh coriander**
       Extra fresh coriander leaves, to garnish

1 To make the spiced coconut pilaf, rinse the rice under cold running water until the water runs clear.

2 Heat 2 tsp vegetable oil in a medium saucepan over medium heat. Add the almonds and stir for 5 minutes or until golden. Remove almonds from the pan with a slotted spoon and drain on absorbent paper.

3 Add the remaining vegetable oil to the saucepan and heat over medium-high heat. Add the onion and cook for 10–15 minutes or until lightly golden. Reduce heat to medium, add the garlic, ginger, cinnamon, cardamom seeds, cloves and chilli powder and stir for 1–2 minutes or until aromatic.

4 Add the rinsed rice to the saucepan and stir over medium heat for 2–3 minutes or until the rice is coated with oil and spices and is lightly toasted. Add the stock, coconut milk and the salt, stir, increase heat to high and bring to the boil. Reduce heat to low, cover and simmer gently for 15 minutes or until all the liquid has been absorbed.

5 Meanwhile, combine the cumin with the salt and sprinkle over the lamb cutlets on both sides. Brush a chargrill or barbecue grill with a little vegetable oil to grease and preheat on medium-high. Cook the lamb cutlets for 2 minutes each side for medium, or until cooked to your liking. Remove from the pan and keep warm.

6 Remove the saucepan with the rice from the heat. Remove the lid and sprinkle the currants over the rice. Cover with the lid and stand for 3–5 minutes. Sprinkle the coriander over the rice and then stir with a fork to separate the grains and evenly distribute the currants and coriander through the rice.

7 Serve the lamb cutlets accompanied by the rice sprinkled with the almonds, extra coriander and the lemon wedges.

Steaming is the best way to retain the goodness and bring out the natural flavours of foods. Lemon grass and ginger give this fish a fresh, spicy flavour. Serve it with steamed Asian greens and jasmine rice. You will need an inexpensive 30cm (12 in) bamboo steamer with one tier for this recipe.

steamed fish
with ginger & lemon grass

serves: 2   prep: 15 mins   cooking: 8–10 mins

2	300g (1/2 pound) scaled, cleaned and gutted baby snapper
	Salt, to taste
2 tsp	sesame oil
1	5cm (2 in) piece fresh ginger, peeled, cut into fine strips
1	lemon grass stem, pale section only, thinly sliced diagonally
4	green shallots, trimmed, thinly sliced diagonally

soy garlic sauce

60mls	(1/4 cup) soy sauce
1 tbs	peanut oil
1 1/2 tsp	fish sauce
2	garlic cloves, finely chopped

1 Wash the cleaned and gutted fish and wipe inside and out with paper towel to dry well. Trim the fins with poultry scissors if desired. Use a sharp knife to cut 3 slashes in the thickest part of the flesh on both sides of each fish. Rub both sides of the fish with a little salt and then the sesame oil.

2 Sprinkle half the ginger and lemon grass evenly over a 30cm (12 in) plate. Place the scored fish on top and sprinkle with remaining ginger, lemon grass and the green shallots.

3 Bring about 5cm of water to the boil in a medium wok or a saucepan that allows the steamer to fit comfortably into the rim without falling inside. Reduce heat to medium-high so the water is held at a gentle, not rolling, boil.

4 Place the plated fish into the steaming basket. Place steaming basket over the boiling water (make sure the bottom of the steaming basket doesn't touch the water). Cover the basket tightly with the lid. (If the lid doesn't seal well, place a clean cotton tea towel over the steamer basket before covering with the lid.) Steam the fish for 8–10 minutes or until the fish is just cooked through and flakes when tested with a fork at the thickest part. Remove the basket from the wok or saucepan immediately.

5 Meanwhile, to make the soy garlic sauce, combine the soy sauce, peanut oil, fish sauce and garlic in a small bowl and mix well.

6 Transfer the cooked fish to serving plates with any juices that have collected on the steaming plate. Spoon the soy garlic sauce over the fish and serve.

microwave fish curry

serves: 4-6 prep: 15 mins (plus 5 mins standing time) cooking: 15 mins

2 tsp vegetable oil
2 tsp finely chopped or grated fresh ginger
2 garlic cloves, finely chopped
1 small brown onion, finely diced
1 tbs Thai green curry paste, or to taste
1 400ml can coconut cream
2 tsp sugar
Salt & ground black pepper, to taste
600g (1¹/₂ pounds) thick, firm white fish fil lets (like lingor gemfish), deboned, cut into large chunks
¹/₂ bunch English spinach, stems washed, trimmed, leaves coarsely shredded
1 tbs fish sauce
2 tbs fresh coriander leaves
Cooked jasmine rice, to serve

1 Place oil, ginger and garlic in a large, heat-resistant, microwave-safe dish. Heat, uncovered, for 1 minute on High/850watts/100%. Add the onion and cook for 1 minute on High/850watts/100%.

2 Add curry paste, stir well and cook for 2 minutes on High/850watts/100%. Pour in the coconut cream and mix well. Cook for 2–3 minutes on Medium-High/650watts/70% or until the mixture simmers. Stir in the sugar and season with salt and pepper.

3 Add the fish and cook for 4–5 minutes on Medium/500watts/50%.

4 Stir gently, so as not to break up the fish, then add the spinach and the fish sauce. Return to the microwave and cook for another 2 minutes on Medium/500watts/50%. Check to see if the fish is just cooked. It should be opaque and the flesh should flake when tested with a fork, but remember that it will continue to cook in the hot sauce after it is removed from the microwave.

5 Remove the dish from the microwave, cover and stand for 5 minutes. Sprinkle with the coriander leaves and serve with the jasmine rice.

Shiitake mushrooms are similar but more delicate-looking than the common

mushroom, and they have an earthy, almost meaty, flavour and a deep-brown coloured cap.

When you buy them make sure they are firm and dry. This is the best indicator of freshness.

ginger beef stir-fry with shiitake mushrooms & noodles

serves: 4 prep: 20 mins cooking: 10 min

200g	(1 cup) dried egg noodles
2 tbs	sesame seeds
2 tbs	peanut oil
500g	(1 pound) piece beef fillet or rump, cut into 2cm-/1 in-thick steaks, then cut across the grain into thin strips
5cm	(2 in) piece fresh ginger, peeled, cut into thin sticks
115g	(1 tray) fresh baby corn, halved lengthways
200g	(1 cup) shiitake mushrooms, stems trimmed
1	lemon grass stem, pale section only, bruised, finely sliced
200g	(1 cup) snow peas, topped
1¹/₂ tbs	oyster sauce
3 tsp	fish sauce
1¹/₂ tbs	fresh lemon or lime juice
2 tbs	water
¹/₂	bunch green shallots, diagonally sliced
1	bunch fresh coriander, leaves picked

1 Cook the noodles in a large saucepan of salted boiling water, following packet directions, until tender. Drain and set aside.

2 Heat a wok over medium heat. Add the sesame seeds and toss for 1–2 minutes or until toasted. Remove from the wok and set aside.

3 Heat the wok over high heat for about 1 minute. Add 1 tbs of the peanut oil and heat for 30–60 seconds or until hot. Add half the beef strips and half the ginger and stir-fry for 30 seconds or until the beef is just sealed. Remove the beef and ginger from the wok with a slotted spoon and transfer to a plate. Add about half the remaining oil and stir-fry the remaining beef strips and ginger.

4 Add the remaining oil to the wok and heat for 30–60 seconds or until hot. Add the corn and stir-fry for 1 minute. Add the mushrooms and lemon grass and stir-fry for a further 1 minute. Add the snow peas, oyster sauce, fish sauce, lemon or lime juice and water. Cook, tossing well, for 1 minute or until the snow peas are tender crisp.

5 Return the beef to the wok with the green shallots, coriander leaves and the noodles and toss to combine. Serve immediately, sprinkled with the toasted sesame seeds.

Both the Middle East and India lay claim to pilaf. This pilaf uses plenty of fresh herbs and watercress to give it a fresh 'green' flavour.

green pilaf

serves: 4 as a light meal, 6 as an accompaniment prep: 15 mins (plus 5 mins standing time) cooking: 20–25 mins

300g	(1$\frac{1}{2}$ cups) basmati rice
2 tbs	olive oil
2	medium leeks, sliced, washed
1 tsp	freshly ground or grated nutmeg
625mls	(2$\frac{1}{2}$ cups) vegetable or chicken stock
	Pinch of salt, or to taste
1	small bunch watercress, washed, leaves picked
$\frac{1}{2}$ cup	chopped fresh continental parsley
$\frac{1}{3}$ cup	chopped fresh mint
	Shaved parmesan, to serve
	Ground black pepper, to taste

1 Rinse the basmati rice under cold running water until the water runs clear.

2 Heat olive oil in a medium saucepan over medium heat and cook leeks for 5 minutes or until soft. Add nutmeg and cook for a further 1 minute or until aromatic. Add the rinsed rice and stir over medium heat for 1–2 minutes or until coated with oil and lightly toasted.

3 Add the stock and salt and stir to combine. Increase heat to high and bring to the boil. Reduce the heat to low, cover and simmer gently for 15 minutes or until the liquid has been absorbed.

4 Remove the saucepan from the heat, remove the lid and sprinkle the watercress, parsley and mint over the rice. Cover with the lid and stand for 5 minutes.

5 Stir the rice with a fork to separate the grains and evenly distribute the watercress and herbs through the rice. Serve topped with parmesan and sprinkled with pepper.

oriental roast chicken

serves: 4 prep: 10 mins cooking: 60–70 mins

1	1.6kg (3 pounds) chicken
60mls	(1/4 cup) soy sauce
2 tbs	black bean sauce
1 tsp	sesame oil
1	small fresh red chilli, deseeded, finely sliced
2 tsp	grated fresh ginger
	Steamed halved baby bok choy, to serve
	Cooked long-grain rice to serve

1 Preheat oven to 180°C (350°F).

2 Briefly rinse the chicken cavity and pat dry all over with paper towel.

3 Combine the soy sauce, black bean sauce, sesame oil, chilli and ginger in a small bowl and mix well. Rub some of the soy sauce marinade evenly over the chicken, covering all the skin.

4 Place the chicken, breast side down, in a roasting pan. Roast in preheated oven for 30 minutes, basting occasionally with the remaining marinade.

5 Remove the roasting pan from the oven, turn the chicken over and spoon any cooking juices over the top. Return to the oven and roast for a further 30–40 minutes, basting occasionally, or until the chicken is just cooked through and the skin is crisp and golden.

6 Remove the chicken from the roasting pan and place on a serving platter. Strain any cooking juices that have gathered in the bottom of the pan. Serve the chicken with the cooking juices spooned over and accompanied by the bok choy and the rice.

octopus with olives & rocket

serves: 6 as an entree, 4 as a main   prep: 30 mins (plus 10 mins cooling time)   cooking: 20 mins

2 red capsicum (peppers), quartered, deseeded
8 (about 500g) baby octopus, prepared (see note)
2 red onions, quartered
   Olive oil, for brushing
1/2 bunch rocket, trimmed, washed
100g (1/2 cup) kalamata olives
2 garlic cloves, finely chopped
2 tbs chopped fresh continental parsley
2 tbs extra virgin olive oil
   Salt & ground black pepper, to taste
   Crusty bread, to serve

1 Preheat grill on high.
2 Place capsicum, skin side up, under preheated grill and cook for 8–10 minutes or until charred and blistered. Transfer to a sealed plastic bag and stand for 10 minutes (this helps lift the skin). Remove the skin from the capsicum and cut the flesh into thin strips. Place into a large bowl.
3 Leave the grill on or preheat a chargrill on high. Brush the octopus and onions with the olive oil and cook under preheated grill or on chargrill, turning once during cooking, for 5–7 minutes or until onion is starting to brown and octopus is just cooked through. (To test if the octopus is cooked, cut at the thickest part and, if ready, it should no longer be translucent.)
4 Add the octopus, onions, rocket, olives, garlic, parsley, olive oil and salt and pepper to the capsicum in the bowl. Toss to combine. Serve warm or at room temperature with crusty bread.

note: to prepare octopus for cooking, cut tentacles from the body with a sharp knife. Use your fingers to locate and remove the hard 'beak' where the tentacles meet. Make a slit down one side of the head, turn inside out and remove internal organs and the ink sac. Clean with damp paper towel, trim and cut into desired portions.

Serve this puree as you would mashed potato—as an accompaniment to roasted or grilled meats and vegetables.

chickpea & garlic puree

serves: 4 prep: 5-10 mins cooking: 5 mins

300mls (1^1/$_3$ cups) thin cream
50g (2^1/$_2$ tbs) butter
3 300g (1^1/$_2$ cups) cans chickpeas, rinsed, drained
4 garlic cloves, crushed
Sea salt & ground black pepper, to taste

1 Heat cream in a small saucepan over medium heat until just simmering. Keep warm.

2 Meanwhile, melt the butter in a frying pan over medium heat. Add chickpeas and garlic and cook, stirring occasionally, for 5 minutes or until heated through.

3 Reserve about 1 tbs of the chickpea mixture. Transfer the remaining mixture to the bowl of a food processor. Add the heated cream and process until smooth. Season with salt and pepper.

4 Serve the warm puree garnished with the reserved chickpeas and sprinkled with a little salt and pepper.

Many of us buy it, but baked ricotta is one of the easiest things to make. It will keep in plastic wrap in the fridge for up to 2 days. Bring it to room temperature to serve. Tomatoes, mushrooms and prosciutto make good brunch accompaniments.

baked ricotta with thyme

serves: 8 prep: 5 mins cooking: 20 mins

Extra virgin olive oil
1   bunch fresh thyme, tough stalk ends trimmed
1 kg fresh ricotta
Salt & ground black pepper, to taste

1 Preheat oven to 200°C (400°F). Brush a shallow round 18cm (7 in) cake pan with the olive oil to grease.
2 Reserve 8 sprigs of the fresh thyme for garnish. Place remaining thyme over the base of the cake pan. Press the ricotta firmly into the pan over the thyme. Drizzle evenly with 1 tbs of olive oil and then sprinkle with salt and pepper to taste.
3 Bake ricotta in preheated oven for 20 minutes or until firm and browned around the edges.
4 Serve warm or at room temperature topped with leaves from reserved thyme sprigs and drizzled with a little more olive oil.

roasted tomatoes

serves: 8 prep: 5 mins cooking: 45 mins

8   egg tomatoes, halved lengthways
3 tsp extra virgin olive oil
1   bunch fresh oregano
Salt & ground black pepper, to taste

1 Preheat oven to 150°C (300°F).
2 Place tomatoes, cut side up, on a baking tray lined with non-stick baking paper. Drizzle with the oil and then sprinkle with the oregano leaves, salt and pepper.
3 Roast in preheated oven for 45 minutes. Serve warm or at room temperature.

chargrilled mushrooms

serves: 8 prep: 5 mins cooking: 5–8 mins

2 tbs olive oil
1 tbs balsamic vinegar
1   garlic clove, crushed
16   medium mushroom flats, stalks trimmed
Salt & ground black pepper, to taste

1 Preheat chargrill over medium-high heat.
2 Combine the olive oil, balsamic vinegar and garlic in a bowl and whisk to combine.
3 Brush the mushrooms with the oil mixture and season with salt and pepper. Cook the mushrooms on preheated chargrill for 4 minutes each side or until tender. Serve warm or at room temperature.

crispy grilled prosciutto

serves: 8 cooking: 2–4 mins

8   prosciutto slices

1 Preheat grill on high.
2 Place prosciutto on a grill tray or baking tray and cook under preheated grill for 1–2 minutes each side or until crisp.

You can make this sauce to sell at spring fêtes and fundraisers. It makes a large quantity and if bottled correctly will store in a cool, dark cupboard for up to 12 months (see note below about sterilising the bottles). Once opened, keep the sauce in the fridge for 6-8 weeks.

old fashioned tomato sauce

makes: about 2 litres (8 cups)   prep: 10 mins (plus 10 mins cooling time)   cooking: 70 mins

60mls	(¹/₄ cup) olive oil
2	brown onions, coarsely chopped
2	medium red capsicum (peppers), deseeded, coarsely chopped
8	garlic cloves, peeled, coarsely chopped
4	celery stalks, coarsely chopped
1 tsp	dried basil
6	400g (16 oz) cans whole peeled tomatoes, undrained
200mls	(³/₄ cup) white wine vinegar
110g	(¹/₂ cup) sugar
2 tsp	salt

1 Heat the olive oil in a very large saucepan over high heat. Add the onions and cook, stirring occasionally, for 5 minutes until soft. Add the capsicum, garlic, celery and basil and cook, stirring occasionally, for a further 5 minutes or until aromatic.

2 Add the undrained tomatoes, vinegar, sugar and salt and stir until combined. Cover and bring to the boil over high heat. Reduce heat and simmer, uncovered, stirring occasionally, for 1 hour or until reduced and thickened to a good sauce consistency. Remove saucepan from the heat. Stand for 10 minutes to cool slightly.

3 Transfer one third of the tomato mixture to a blender or the bowl of a food processor and process until smooth. Transfer to a clean saucepan. Repeat with remaining tomato mixture.

4 Bring the sauce back to the boil over high heat.

5 Pour the hot sauce into hot sterilised bottles (see note). Seal immediately and invert bottles for 2 minutes. Stand bottles upright and cool to room temperature, then label and date.

note: to sterilise bottles, wash the bottles, rubber seals and lids in warm, soapy water and rinse well. Place bottles and lids in a large saucepan and cover with water. Bring to the boil and boil for 10 minutes. Transfer bottles to a baking tray lined with baking paper and place in preheated oven at 100°C (220°CF) until dry. Air-dry the lids and rubber seals. Use the bottles straight from the oven.

ROCKET

■ For my favourite "cooking for one" dish, toss a handful of rocket with 2 tsp drained capers, a flaked drained small can of tuna in oil, 2 tsp of the oil from the tuna and juice from ¹/₂ lemon in a small saucepan over medium heat until the rocket wilts. Toss through cooked pasta of your choice (shells are good) and season with lots of salt and ground black pepper.

■ Make a sandwich of rocket, tomato and avocado on a crusty white bread roll with good quality mayo and lots of salt and ground black pepper.

■ Toss 4 medium red onions, cut into eighths with about 1 tbs olive oil and roast in an oven preheated to 200°C (400°F) for 20 minutes. Combine the roasted onion with 150g (1 cup) rocket and 100g (5 tbs) shaved Parmesan. Then drizzle with a dressing made by combining 3 tbs extra virgin olive oil, 1¹/₂ tbs balsamic vinegar, 1 garlic clove, finely chopped and salt and black pepper to taste. Serves 4-6 as an accompaniment.

good rocket partners: balsamic vinegar, tomatoes, salt, garlic, olive oil, Parmesan, fish, roasted capsicum (pepper), lemon.

strawberry coconut cake

serves: 12   prep: 20 mins (plus 1 hour standing and cooling time)   cooking: 30–35 mins

Melted butter or margarine, for greasing

1	270ml can (1 cup) coconut milk
135g	(1¹/₂ cups) desiccated coconut
200g	butter, at room temperature
295g	(1¹/₃ cups) caster sugar
4	eggs
250g	(1²/₃ cups) self-raising flour, sifted

filling

170g	(¹/₂ cup) strawberry jam
125mls	(¹/₂ cup) sour cream

topping

250g	(1 punnet) small strawberries, hulled, if desired
	Icing sugar, to decorate

1 Preheat oven to 180°C (350°F). Brush two round 20cm (8 in) shallow cake pans with the melted butter or margarine to grease. Line the base of each pan with non-stick baking paper.

2 Combine the coconut milk and coconut in a small saucepan and bring to a simmer over medium heat. Remove from heat, transfer to a bowl and cool to room temperature. (See microwave tip.)

3 Use electric beaters to beat butter and caster sugar in a large mixing bowl until pale and creamy. Add eggs one at a time and beat well after each addition until combined.

4 Use a large metal spoon to fold a large spoonful of flour into the butter mixture. Fold in the cooled coconut mixture and then the remaining flour until combined. Divide mixture evenly between the prepared pans and smooth the surfaces.

5 Bake in preheated oven for 25–30 minutes or until golden and cooked when a skewer inserted into the centre of the cakes comes out clean. Stand in pans for 10 minutes. Run a knife around the edge of the cakes and then turn them onto wire racks to cool.

6 To assemble, place one cake layer on a serving plate and spread evenly with the strawberry jam and then the sour cream. Top with remaining cake layer. Decorate with strawberries and dust liberally with the icing sugar.

microwave tip: combine the coconut milk and coconut in a medium, heat-resistant microwave-safe bowl. Heat, uncovered, for 2–3 minutes on Medium/500watts/50%. Cool.

This recipe, with a touch of mint, makes enough syrup for 20 glasses of old-fashioned lemonade. Take it on picnics or sip it in the sun on spring afternoons. It will store in the fridge for up to 1 month.

homemade lemonade

makes: about 750mls (3 cups) base syrup   prep: 10 mins (plus 1 hour cooling time)   cooking: 5 mins

3   sprigs fresh mint
220g   (1 cup) sugar
375mls (1½ cups) fresh lemon juice
250mls (1 cup) water
        Lemon slices (optional), to serve
        Chilled water, sparkling mineral
        water or soda water, to serve

1 Press the mint sprigs with the flat of a knife to lightly crush the leaves.
2 Combine the mint, sugar, lemon juice and water in a medium saucepan. Stir over medium heat until the sugar dissolves. (See microwave tip.)
3 Remove the saucepan from the heat. Discard the mint sprigs and set the syrup aside for about 1 hour or until cooled.
4 Pour the syrup into clean, airtight bottles, seal and store in the fridge.
5 To serve, pour a little into a glass, add a slice of lemon, if using, and top with water, mineral water or soda water.

microwave tip: combine mint, sugar, lemon juice and water in a medium, heat-resistant microwave-safe bowl or jug. Cover with a lid or plastic wrap and cook for 2–3 minutes on High/850watts/100% or until sugar dissolves, stir once during cooking.

The velvety texture of mousse is captured in this frozen dessert. It is wickedly rich. If you like, the mixture can be frozen in six 250mls (1 cup) ramekins to make individual servings.

frozen chocolate mousse

serves: 6 (makes 1.5 litres/6 cups) prep: 10 mins (plus 20 mins cooling and 4–6 hours freezing time) cooking: 10 mins

300g	(11 oz) good-quality dark chocolate, coarsely chopped
250mls	(1 cup) thickened cream
6	eggs, separated
1 tbs	caster sugar
100g	(²/₃ cup) hazelnuts, to serve

1 Place the chocolate and 125mls (¹/₂ cup) cream in a medium heat-resistant bowl or in the top of a double saucepan and stir over simmering water until the chocolate has melted and the mixture is smooth. (See microwave tip 1.) Set aside until cooled almost to room temperature.

2 Use electric beaters to whisk the egg yolks and caster sugar in a large bowl until pale and creamy. Stir in the chocolate mixture until well combined.

3 Use clean electric beaters or a hand whisk to whisk the remaining cream in a separate, medium bowl until soft peaks form. Use a large metal spoon to fold the cream into the chocolate mixture until just combined.

4 Again, use clean electric beaters or a hand whisk to whisk the egg whites in a separate, clean, medium bowl until soft peaks form. Fold the egg whites into the chocolate mixture until combined.

5 Pour the mixture into an airtight container. Freeze for 4–6 hours or until firm.

6 Meanwhile, preheat the oven to 180°C (350°F). Place the hazelnuts on a baking tray and toast in preheated oven for 10 minutes or until aromatic. (See microwave tip 2.) Cool and then roughly chop.

7 To serve, scoop the frozen chocolate mousse into bowls, sprinkle with the toasted hazelnuts and serve immediately.

microwave tip 1: place the chocolate and 125ml (¹/₂ cup) cream in a medium heat-resistant, microwave-safe bowl and heat, uncovered, for 2–3 minutes on Medium-High/650watts/70%, stirring every minute, or until the chocolate has melted and the mixture is smooth.

microwave tip 2: place the hazelnuts in an oven bag. Twist bag opening to seal and then place the bag directly onto the turntable. Cook for 3–5 minutes on High/850watts/100%, gently shaking the bag every minute. Stand until cool. The nuts will darken on standing.

I grew up on homemade biscuits and this recipe brings back fond memories.
It is a good one for the kids, especially when shaping the dough and making the
holes for the jam. The biscuits will store in an airtight jar for up to a week.

jam drops

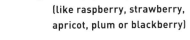

makes: about 40   prep: 20 mins   cooking: 18–20 mins (per batch)

125g (6 tbs) butter
 75g (^{1}/3 cup) caster sugar
1 tsp vanilla essence
185g (1^1/4 cups) plain flour
1 tsp baking powder
2 tbs milk
170g (^{1}/3 cup) jam of your choice
       (like raspberry, strawberry,
       apricot, plum or blackberry)

HONEY

- Beat 250g (1^2/3 cups) ricotta with 3 tbs thickened cream and 2 tbs honey with a wooden spoon until smooth. Serve spoonfuls drizzled with a little honey and accompanied by fresh dates or strawberries.
- When making homemade muesli toss rolled oats with a little warmed honey to sweeten.
- Marinate chicken pieces or a whole chicken in a mixture of 2 parts light soy sauce, 1 part honey and finely chopped garlic and ginger to taste before cooking.

good honey partners: pecans, walnuts, soy sauce, ricotta, cream, pears, bananas, hot buttered crumpets and toast, iced lemon tea, pork, lamb, ginger, cinnamon.

1 Preheat oven to 180°C (350°F). Line a baking tray with non-stick baking paper.
2 Use electric beaters to beat the butter, sugar and vanilla essence in a medium mixing bowl until pale and creamy.
3 Sift together the plain flour and baking powder. Add the dry ingredients and milk to the butter mixture. Mix to a soft dough with a wooden spoon.
4 Roll small balls of the biscuit dough with lightly floured hands and place on the prepared baking tray about 5cm (2 in) apart. Flatten each ball with a spatula to make them 3.5cm (1.5 in) in diameter. Make a 2cm (1 in)-wide indent in the centre of each with your finger or the end of a wooden spoon. Fill each indent generously with jam.
5 Bake in preheated oven for 18–20 minutes or until lightly golden and cooked through. Stand on baking tray for 2–3 minutes before transferring to a wire rack to cool. Repeat with the remaining biscuit dough and jam.

chocolate cake

serves: 6   prep: 20 mins   cooking: 45 mins

	Melted butter or margarine, for greasing
50g	(¹/₂ cup) cocoa powder
125mls	(¹/₂ cup) boiling water
125g	(6 tbs) butter, at room temperature
275g	(1¹/₄ cups) caster sugar
1 tsp	vanilla essence
3	eggs
150g	(1 cup) self-raising flour
40g	(¹/₄ cup) plain flour
	Icing sugar, to serve

1 Preheat oven to 180°C (350°F). Brush a deep 22cm (8.5 in) round cake pan with the melted butter or margarine to grease and then line the base with non-stick baking paper.

2 Sift cocoa powder into bowl. Gradually add almost all the water, stirring to form a smooth, thick paste. Stir in remaining water. Set aside.

3 Use electric beaters to beat the butter, caster sugar and vanilla essence in a medium mixing bowl for 1–2 minutes or until pale. Add the eggs one at a time, beating well after each until combined.

4 Sift together the flours. Use a large metal spoon to fold the flours into the butter mixture alternately with the cocoa mixture, in 2 batches each, until combined. Spoon the mixture into the prepared cake pan and smooth the surface with the back of the spoon.

5 Bake in preheated oven for 45 minutes or until a skewer inserted into the centre of the cake comes out clean. Stand for 3 minutes before turning out onto a wire rack to cool. Serve dusted with icing sugar.

This icy dessert infused with mint is perfect to serve after an Asian-inspired meal. It will store in your freezer for up to 4 weeks. Just scrape a fork through it to break up the ice crystals before serving. An instant refresher.

pineapple & mint granita

serves: 8 (makes about 1.75 litres/7 cups)   prep: 20 mins (plus 4–5 hours freezing time)

1	medium (about 1.25kg) pineapple
220g	(1 cup) sugar
160mls	($^2/_3$ cup) unsweetened pineapple juice
750mls	(3 cups) water
80mls	($^1/_3$ cup) fresh lemon juice
1$^1/_4$ tbs	coarsely chopped fresh mint
	Extra fresh mint leaves, to decorate

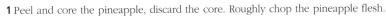

1 Peel and core the pineapple, discard the core. Roughly chop the pineapple flesh.

2 Place 600g (4 cups) of the pineapple flesh into a food processor, add the sugar and process until almost smooth. (Reserve any remaining pineapple for another use.) Add the pineapple juice, water and lemon juice to the pineapple puree and process until just combined (you may have to do this in two separate batches).

3 Pour the pineapple mixture into a 2-litre (8-cup) airtight container and stir through the chopped mint. Cover and freeze for 2 hours or until partially set.

4 Flake the mixture with a fork to break up the ice crystals and refreeze for a further 2–3 hours or until completely frozen. Flake with a fork again to break up the ice crystals. Return the granita to the freezer until required.

5 Thirty minutes before serving, flake the granita with a fork to break into ice crystals and return to the freezer. Place individual serving glasses in the freezer for 15 minutes to chill thoroughly. Spoon the granita into the chilled serving glasses, decorate with the extra mint leaves and serve immediately.

BANANAS

■ Add sliced banana to a pan of frothing butter, sprinkle with brown sugar and cook over medium heat until the banana is coated with the caramel. Add a splash of brandy and serve warm over vanilla ice-cream.

■ For a banana smoothie, blend a ripe banana, 185mls ($^3/_4$ cup) milk, a few spoonfuls of natural yoghurt, a spoonful of honey, 1 tsp vanilla essence and $^1/_2$ tsp ground cinnamon. Serves 1.

■ Place whole or sliced banana on a piece of foil. Drizzle with maple or golden syrup and a little thickened cream, wrap up and cook on preheated barbecue for 10-15 minutes or until soft and heated through.

good banana partners: brown sugar, honey, maple syrup, golden syrup, pecan nuts, toast, coconut, sultanas, cinnamon, vanilla, chocolate.

summer

a season for making memories

Summer is my favourite season. It's funny, isn't it, how summer dominates our childhood memories?

I remember huge wedges of watermelon filled with juice

that trickled down our chins. It was the summer fruit that refreshed us between games of tennis and dips in the water during the endless school holidays. Watermelon also provided ammunition for our seed-spitting competitions. And it was in summer at the beach that we caught prawns on their way out to sea on moonless nights and fished for flathead in the early mornings.

Summer reminds me of Dad's corn 'forest' that produced the sweetest corn I have ever tasted, the climbing bean vines that grew up our back fence and the wonderful Tommy Toe

tomatoes that we popped in our mouths whole. Their intense flavour exploded once we broke the skin with our teeth—better than any lolly!

Summer also evokes the seriously strawberry-flavoured ice-cream I used to make with my Aunt Jean with fruit straight from her patch; the boxes and boxes of plums we gathered from the tree in the corner of Mum's garden (and the jam I started to make with them once I was shown how at college); and the annual box of cherries delivered to our door by one of our next-door-neighbours' contract shearers in exchange for a daily sponge cake during his working stay. It was the best deal our family ever made!

Nowadays I'm a city slicker, and summer brings watermelon

granita (see p 86) made for lazy Sunday lunches in our sunny courtyard. It means the rocket that shares a patch with parsley, mint, basil, chives and oregano, and revels in the warmer weather.

Summer is about white peaches that appear in the stores towards the middle of the season and the yellow ones that are so juicy they leave 'I've been here' spots on freshly washed t-shirts. And it's the wonderful array of berries that beg to be combined in my own homemade ice-cream (see p 91).

I only wish the fruits of summer would hold their form for weeks when arranged in a bowl on a bench, to be admired for their beautiful shapes, heavenly scents and stunning colours. Alas, once ripe, they last longer if stored in the fridge.

I trust and hope that the recipes I've included will help you create your own summer memories.

summer's best
a guide to help you use produce at the height of its season

vegetables

- **Asian greens:**
  bok choy (early)
  choy sum (early)
  Chinese cabbage
  (wong nga bok)
- **asparagus** (early)
- **beans:**
  butter
  green
  Italian flat
  snake (late)
- **capsicum (peppers)**
- **celery** (early to mid)
- **chillies**
- **corn**
- **cucumber**
- **eggplant**
- **garlic**
- **lettuce**
- **mushrooms (cultivated)**
- **okra** (mid to late)
- **onions:**
  brown
  green shallots/green onions/
  scallions
  French shallots/eshallots
  red/Spanish
  spring
  white
- **peas:**
  green
- **potatoes (general)**
- **pumpkin**
- **radish**
- **rhubarb** (early)
- **squash** (mid to late)
- **tomatoes**
- **witlof**
- **zucchini**

This information may vary slightly depending on
where you live and/or weather conditions

fruit

- **apples:**
  jonathan (late)
  royal gala (late)
- **apricots** (early to mid)
- **avocados** (late)
- **bananas**
- **berries:**
  blackberries
  blackcurrants, red currants &
  white currants (early to mid)
  blueberries (early to mid)
  boysenberries
  loganberries (early)
  raspberries (early to mid)
  strawberries
- **cherries** (early to mid)
- **figs** (late)
- **grapefruit**
  pink (early)
- **grapes**
- **lychees**
- **mangoes**
- **melons:**
  honeydew
  rockmelon (cantaloupe)
  watermelon
- **nectarines**
- **oranges**
  valencia
- **papaya**
- **passionfruit** (mid to late)
- **pawpaw**
- **peaches**
- **pears**
  williams (late)
- **pineapple**
- **plums** (mid to late)
- **rambutans** (mid to late)

This is the best starter when entertaining in summer.

The salsa can be made up to 2 hours ahead and kept in your

fridge ready to spoon over the oysters.

fresh oysters with mango & red capsicum salsa

serves: 8 as a starter or 4 as an entree   prep: 15 mins

24   oysters, on their half shell

mango & red capsicum salsa
- 1   ripe mango, peeled, flesh removed
- 1   red capsicum (pepper), quartered, deseeded
- 1   medium red onion
- 1/4 cup   chopped fresh coriander
- 1 tbs   fresh lime juice, or to taste

1 To make the salsa, finely dice the mango, capsicum and onion. Combine the mango, capsicum, onion, coriander and lime juice in a bowl.

2 Serve each oyster topped with a spoonful of the salsa.

spaghetti with fried capers & smoked salmon

serves: 4   prep: 10 mins   cooking: 15 mins

500g	(1 pound) dried spaghetti
100g	($^1/_2$ cup) drained capers
125mls	($^1/_2$ cup) vegetable oil, for frying
1 tbs	olive oil
1	red onion, thinly sliced
2	garlic cloves, finely chopped
200g	(7 oz) thinly sliced smoked salmon, cut into 2cm-wide strips
1 tbs	fresh thyme leaves
	Ground black pepper, to taste
	Olive oil, extra, for serving

1 Cook spaghetti in a large saucepan of salted boiling water following packet directions or until al dente.

2 Meanwhile rinse the capers under cold running water then drain and pat dry with paper towel.

3 Heat the vegetable oil in a small saucepan over medium heat until hot. Gently fry the capers in 3 separate batches in the hot oil for 30-60 seconds or until the buds begin to open and are lightly brown. Remove the capers from the pan with a slotted spoon and drain on paper towel.

4 Heat the olive oil in a large saucepan over medium heat and cook the red onion for 5 minutes or until soft. Add the garlic and cook for 1 minute.

5 Drain the cooked pasta and add to the saucepan with the capers, smoked salmon and thyme. Toss quickly in the pan for about 1 minute being careful not to overheat the salmon. Season with pepper.

6 Divide among serving bowls, drizzle with a little extra olive oil, and serve.

OLIVE OIL

■ Make pesto by processing 1 cup firmly packed fresh basil leaves, 3 garlic cloves and 3 tbs pine nuts in a food processor until combined. Gradually add enough olive oil (about 4–5 tbs) to form a thin smooth paste. Stir in 3 tbs freshly grated Parmesan and season well with salt and ground black pepper. Serve with pasta, spread on bread and top with sliced tomato or use to accompany barbecued chicken or fish.

■ Rub king edward, russet burbank (idaho) or sebago (brushed) potatoes that have been cut into wedges with olive oil and salt. Roast in oven pre-heated to 200°C (400°F) until crisp and golden.

■ To make a quick vinaigrette for a salad of baby spinach, green beans and oven dried tomatoes (see p 68) whisk together 2 tbs red wine vinegar, 2 large garlic cloves finely chopped, 1 tsp Dijon mustard and salt and pepper to taste. Gradually whisk in 125mls ($^1/_2$ cup) olive oil.

■ Don't forget olive oil spray to lightly grease foil, your barbecue grill or chargrill.

good olive oil partners: bread, tomatoes, pasta, potatoes, garlic, seafood, chicken, salad leaves, fresh herbs.

You really can't beat fresh corn. If you make these fritters slightly smaller they make wonderful finger food served with some sweet chilli sauce for dipping. If you really must, use 140g (1 cup) drained canned or frozen corn kernels instead of the fresh.

corn & ginger fritters

serves: 4 as an entree   prep: 10 mins   cooking: 8 mins

1	large corn cob, husk and silk removed
2 tsp	finely grated fresh ginger
1	small red chilli, deseeded, finely chopped
2 tbs	finely chopped fresh coriander
	Salt & ground black pepper, to taste
2	eggs, lightly whisked
50g	(¹/₃ cup) plain flour
	Vegetable or canola oil, for frying
1	lime, quartered, to serve
	Extra fresh coriander (optional), to garnish

1 Use a sharp knife to remove the kernels from the corn cob, cutting lengthways close to the cob.

2 Combine the kernels, ginger, chilli and chopped coriander in a medium bowl. Season with salt and pepper and stir in the eggs. Sift the flour over the corn mixture and use a wooden spoon to stir quickly to combine.

3 Pour enough vegetable or canola oil into a large frying pan to cover the base thoroughly. Place over medium heat until the oil is hot. Make 6 individual fritters by spooning about half the mixture into the pan, flatten each slighly and cook for about 2 minutes on each side or until golden and cooked through. Drain on paper towel, set aside and keep warm. Repeat with remaining corn mixture.

4 Serve warm with the lime wedges and garnished with the extra coriander, if desired.

crumbed veal
with crisp sage & lime

serves: 4 prep: 15 mins cooking: 15 mins

500g (1 pound) veal leg steaks, evenly
flattened, cut into serving size pieces
75g (1/2 cup) plain flour
2 eggs, lightly whisked
90g (1 cup) dried breadcrumbs
2 tbs vegetable oil
60g (3 tbs) butter
300g (1 1/3 cups) green beans, topped
Ground black pepper, to taste
1/2 cup lightly packed fresh sage leaves
2 limes, juiced
1 lime, extra, quartered, to serve

1 Lightly coat the veal steaks with the flour, dip them into the whisked eggs and then coat evenly with the breadcrumbs.

2 Heat 1 tbs of the vegetable oil and 20g (1 tbs) of the butter in a large frying pan over medium-high heat. Add half the veal steaks and cook for 2–3 minutes each side or until golden and just cooked. Drain on paper towel and keep warm. Repeat the process using remaining vegetable oil, 20g (1 tbs) of the remaining butter and the veal.

3 Meanwhile, cook beans in a saucepan of boiling water for 4–5 minutes or until tender crisp. Drain and toss with 2 tsp of the remaining butter and pepper to taste. Keep warm.

4 Wipe out the frying pan using paper towel. Add the remaining 2 tsp butter and melt over medium-high heat. Add the sage leaves and cook, turning often, for 2–3 minutes or until crisp. Drain on paper towel. Add the lime juice to pan, stir well and remove from the heat.

5 To serve, place veal onto plates and drizzle with the hot lime juice. Top with the fried sage and serve accompanied by the beans and extra lime wedges.

This dish was developed as part of a menu for a linen lunch just in time for my mum to use at a party she and a few friends were throwing for a bride-to-be. It is a light, fresh dish with a spicy tang thanks to the lime and chilli.

lime chicken
with cellophane noodles

serves: 8 prep: 45 mins cooking: 15–20 mins

200g	(1/2 pound) cellophane (mung bean) noodles
1 tbs	peanut oil
1.5kg	(about 8) single chicken breast fillets, trimmed
2	red capsicum (pepper)
1	large red onion
1	telegraph cucumber
1	bunch fresh mint
	Lime chilli dressing (recipe right)
80g	(1/2 cup) unsalted roasted peanuts, coarsely chopped, to garnish

1 Preheat oven to 180°C (350°F).
2 Soak cellophane noodles in water for 30 minutes or follow packet directions.
3 Meanwhile, heat the peanut oil in a large frying pan over high heat. Add half the chicken and cook for 2 minutes each side or until golden brown and sealed. Remove the chicken from the pan and place on a baking tray lined with non-stick baking paper. Repeat with the remaining chicken.
4 Cook the sealed chicken in preheated oven for 8–10 minutes or until just cooked through. Transfer the chicken to 2 plates, cover loosely with foil and place in the fridge until required.
5 Quarter and deseed the capsicum and then cut into thin strips. Halve the onion and finely slice. Run a vegetable peeler down the length of the cucumber and peel into long ribbons. Shred half the mint leaves and remove the remaining leaves from their sprigs. Combine the capsicum, onion, cucumber and shredded and whole mint leaves in a large bowl. Cover with plastic wrap and set aside.
6 Drain the cellophane noodles and cook in a large saucepan of boiling water for 5 minutes. Drain in a colander and refresh under cold running water.
7 Cut the chicken fillets diagonally into very thin slices. Add the chicken and cellophane noodles to the vegetable mixture with half the dressing and toss lightly to combine.
8 Transfer the chicken mixture to a large serving bowl or individual serving plates and garnish with the roasted peanuts. Serve the remaining dressing separately.

lime chilli dressing

makes: 375mls (1 1/2 cups) prep: 5 mins

5	limes, juiced
60mls	(1/4 cup) sweet chilli sauce
1 tbs	fish sauce
1 tbs	mirin or dry sherry
1 tbs	brown sugar
2 tsp	sesame oil
125mls	(1/2 cup) vegetable or peanut oil

1 Combine the lime juice, sweet chilli sauce, fish sauce, mirin or dry sherry, brown sugar and sesame oil in a bowl.
2 Gradually whisk in the vegetable or peanut oil until the dressing is well combined and slightly thickened.

lebanese rolls
with minted lamb & tomato

makes: 6   prep: 10–15 mins (plus 10–15 mins resting time)   cooking: 5–10 mins

8 (about 450g) lamb fillets
Olive oil, for brushing
3 large Lebanese bread rounds
180g (²/₃ cup) hummus (see recipe below)
1 bunch fresh mint, leaves picked, coarsely chopped
2 medium ripe tomatoes, cut into 1.5cm pieces
Salt & ground black pepper, to taste

1 Preheat grill on medium-high.

2 Brush the lamb fillets with olive oil and then cook them under preheated grill for 4 minutes each side for medium or until cooked to your liking. Remove from the grill and stand to rest for 10–15 minutes.

3 Split the Lebanese bread rounds in half. Spread each half with the hummus and then roll each into a cone shape.

4 Place each cone on a large serviette or a 30cm (12 in) square of greaseproof baking paper, leaving 8cm (3 in) at the bottom. Wrap the serviette or paper around the bread and twist tightly to seal at the bottom.

5 Cut the lamb fillets into thin slices. Combine the lamb, mint leaves and tomatoes in a medium bowl and season with salt and pepper. Fill each roll with the lamb mixture. Serve immediately or keep in an airtight container in the fridge for up to 2 hours.

to make your own 'quick' hummus: combine a drained and rinsed 300g (1¹/₂ cups) can chickpeas, 60mls (¹/₄ cup) olive oil, juice 1 lemon, 2 large garlic cloves, ¹/₂ tsp cumin powder and ¹/₄ tsp chilli powder in the bowl of a food processor and puree until smooth and well combined. Season well with salt and ground black pepper. Use to spread on bread, as a dip for pita chips or as an accompaniment for barbecued lamb or chicken.

TOMATOES

■ Halve egg tomatoes and place on a wire rack over a lined baking tray. Drizzle with a little olive oil and sprinkle with a little salt and sugar. Roast in an oven preheated to 100ºC (220ºF) for 6–8 hours or until semi-dried. Serve on bread, in salads or as part of an antipasto.

■ To peel tomatoes: cut a shallow cross in the base of the tomatoes and then plunge them into boiling water for 15–30 seconds or until the skin starts to come away near the slit. Quickly transfer them to a bowl of cold water and then peel away the skins.

■ For a quick, punchy sauce heat 1 tbs olive oil in a saucepan and cook 1 small red onion, diced, over medium heat for 3 minutes. Add 1 crushed garlic clove and cook for 1 minute. Add 3 medium ripe tomatoes, coarsely chopped, 2 tsp each of balsamic vinegar and brown sugar and ¹/₂ tsp cayenne pepper. Simmer over medium-low heat for 25 minutes or until thick. Season with salt and black pepper. Great for pasta, to serve with chicken, beef or lamb or on hamburgers (see p 27).

good tomato partners: red capsicum, red onion, sea salt, sugar, shellfish, rocket, basil, balsamic vinegar, bocconcini, thyme, mint, garlic, pasta, lamb, fish, chicken, cumin, Parmesan, oregano.

This recipe uses a leg of lamb that has been boned to produce one large, flattish piece of meat (known as 'butterflied leg of lamb') which is perfect for a summer barbecue.

orange & oregano lamb

serves: 8 prep: 10 mins (plus overnight marinating & 70 mins standing time) cooking: 25-30 mins

1.5kg (3 pounds) butterflied leg of lamb
2 tbs dried oregano
5 bay leaves, crushed
1¹/₂ tbs sea salt
2 tsp cracked black pepper
1¹/₂ tbs olive oil
2 oranges, rind finely grated
375mls (1¹/₂ cups) fresh orange juice
60mls (¹/₄ cup) fresh lemon juice
Fresh oregano sprigs (optional), to garnish

1 Trim any excess fat from the lamb, then place a long skewer through each side so it stays flat and holds together.
2 Combine the oregano, bay leaves, salt, pepper and olive oil in a small bowl and mix well. Rub this mixture into the surface of the lamb. Place into a large glass or ceramic dish.
3 Combine the orange rind and juice and lemon juice and then pour it over the lamb. Cover and place in the fridge overnight, turning occasionally.
4 Remove the lamb from the fridge 1 hour before cooking.
5 Preheat barbecue grill or a chargrill on medium-high.
6 Cook lamb on preheated barbecue or chargrill, basting with the reserved marinade frequently and turning once during cooking, for 25–30 minutes for medium-rare or until cooked to your liking.
7 Remove lamb from barbecue and set aside for 10 minutes to rest. Cut into slices across the grain and serve garnished with the fresh oregano, if desired.

barbecued vegetables
serves: 8 prep: 10 mins
cooking: 20-30 mins

3 large corn cobs, husk and silk removed
2 large orange sweet potatoes (kumara)
80mls (¹/₃ cup) balsamic vinegar (optional), to serve

1 Cut the corn cobs into 3cm-thick slices. Peel and cut the sweet potatoes into 2cm-thick slices.
2 Bring a large saucepan of water to the boil. Add the corn and boil for 8–10 minutes or until just tender. Remove the corn with a slotted spoon and refresh under cold running water. Bring the water back to the boil, add the sweet potatoes and boil for 8–10 minutes. Drain the sweet potatoes and refresh under cold running water.
3 Preheat a barbecue grill or a chargrill on medium-high. Cook the corn and sweet potato slices on the barbecue or chargrill for 2–3 minutes each side or until charred and cooked through.
4 Sprinkle the vegetables with the balsamic vinegar, if desired, and serve warm or at room temperature.

The main reason for salting eggplant (or degorging) is to extract

the bitter juices from the flesh, particularly in mature ones.

If your eggplants are young with seeds that are barely noticeable

it is unnecessary to salt them.

baked eggplant
tomato & ricotta

serves: 6   prep: 20 mins (plus 30 mins degorging time)   cooking: 45–50 mins

4	medium (1.5kg) eggplants, cut into 1.5cm ($^1/_2$ in)-thick slices
	Salt, for degorging
60mls	($^1/_4$ cup) olive oil
500g	(2 cups) fresh ricotta
100g	(1$^1/_4$) cups grated Parmesan
	Ground black pepper, to taste
$^1/_4$ cup	chopped fresh basil
1	quantity basic tomato sauce (see recipe p 131)
	Olive oil, for greasing

1 Sprinkle the eggplant slices with salt. Place in a colander and stand for 30 minutes to degorge. Rinse the eggplant slices well under cold running water and then pat dry with paper towel or a clean tea towel.

2 Preheat grill on high.

3 Place some of the eggplant slices on a grill tray or baking tray in a single layer, brush with a little of the olive oil and cook under preheated grill for 3–4 minutes or until browned. Turn the eggplant slices, brush again with the olive oil and cook for a further 4 minutes or until browned and tender. Transfer the cooked slices to a wire rack and repeat with the remaining eggplant slices and olive oil.

4 Meanwhile, combine the ricotta and 40g ($^1/_2$ cup) of the grated Parmesan in a medium bowl and use a wooden spoon to beat until well combined. Season with salt and pepper.

5 Add the basil to the tomato sauce and stir to combine.

6 Preheat oven to 220°C (424°F). Lightly brush a 1.5-litre (6-cup) ovenproof dish with olive oil to grease.

7 Place half the grilled eggplant slices over the base of the greased dish and then spread with half the tomato sauce. Top with the ricotta mixture and remaining eggplant slices. Spread with the remaining tomato sauce and sprinkle evenly with the remaining grated Parmesan.

8 Bake in preheated oven for 20 minutes or until golden on top and heated through. Serve warm or at room temperature.

yoghurt & mango chutney marinated chicken

serves: 6   prep: 10 mins (plus 1 hour marinating & 15 mins standing time)   cooking: 1½ hours

1   1.8kg (size 18) chicken
Olive oil, for greasing

yoghurt & mango chutney marinade
500g   (2 cups) natural yoghurt
120g   (¹/₃ cup) mango chutney
1 tsp   ground turmeric
¹/₂ tsp   ground allspice

1 To make the marinade, combine the yoghurt, mango chutney, turmeric and allspice in a bowl and mix well.

2 Briefly rinse the chicken under cold running water. Drain, then pat dry inside and out with paper towel. Use a spoon to spread the marinade inside the cavity and then evenly over the outside of the chicken to coat it completely.

3 Place the chicken on a plate, cover and place in the fridge for at least 1 hour, preferably overnight, to marinate.

4 Preheat oven to 180°C (350°F).

5 Brush a roasting pan with olive oil to grease. Place the chicken in the pan and roast in preheated oven for 1½ hours or until the juices run clear when the chicken thigh is pierced with a skewer.

6 Remove from oven, cover loosely with foil and stand for 15 minutes before serving.

MANGOES

■ To make a mango sorbet stir 250mls (1 cup) water and 165g (³/₄ cup) sugar in a saucepan over medium heat until the sugar dissolves. Bring to the boil and then remove from heat. Puree the flesh from 3 large, ripe mangoes. Add the sugar syrup and 3 tbs fresh lime juice. Freeze this mixture until almost set. Puree in a food processor until smooth and then return to the freezer until totally frozen. Adorn with more fresh mango slices. Serves 4–6.

■ Combine 110g (¹/₂ cup) sugar with juice of 2 limes, 2 tbs water and 2 lightly crushed cardamom pods in a saucepan and stir over medium heat until sugar dissolves. Bring to the boil and simmer for 5 minutes or until reduced to a syrupy consistency. Pour over the sliced flesh from 4 mangoes and set aside to macerate for 30 minutes. Serve with thick cream or vanilla ice-cream.

■ Toss some diced mango with diced cucumber, a little fresh red chilli, some fresh lime or lemon juice, a little brown sugar and some fresh coriander leaves to make a salsa for seafood, chicken or pork.

good mango partners: raspberries, vanilla ice-cream, crab, citrus, cardamom, coriander.

Morwong is also known as sea bream or simply as
bream. It is a firm-fleshed fish with a fine texture and
is great to chargrill or to barbecue. It also poaches,
fries, steams and bakes well.

seared fish salad

serves: 4   prep: 15 mins   cooking: 15–20 mins

400g	(2 cups) pink fir apple potatoes, peeled, cut into 1.5cm- or $1/2$ in-thick slices
200g	green beans, topped and tailed
2	(1 cup) medium ripe tomatoes, cut into wedges
1	small red onion, peeled, halved, thinly sliced
2 tbs	torn fresh continental parsley leaves
60mls	($1/4$ cup) olive oil
2 tbs	fresh lime or lemon juice
	Salt & ground black pepper, to taste
4	(about 125g each) morwong fillets

1 Cook potatoes in a saucepan of salted boiling water for 8–10 minutes or until tender. (See microwave tip 1.) Drain, refresh under cold running water and then drain well.

2 Meanwhile, cook the beans in a saucepan of boiling water for 3 minutes or until tender crisp. (See microwave tip 2.) Drain, refresh under cold running water and then drain well.

3 Place the potatoes, beans, tomatoes, onion, parsley, 2 tbs of the olive oil, 1 tbs of the lime or lemon juice and salt and pepper to taste in a medium bowl and stir gently to combine.

4 Preheat a chargrill or barbecue on high.

5 Brush the fish fillets with remaining olive oil and rub with salt and pepper. Cook on preheated chargrill or barbecue for 2–3 minutes each side or until fish is just cooked through and it flakes easily when tested with a fork.

6 Sprinkle the fish fillets with the remaining lime or lemon juice. Divide the potato salad among serving plates and then top with the fish. Serve immediately.

microwave tip 1: wash the whole potatoes and pierce each 4 times with a fork. Place the potatoes around the outer edge of the turntable. Cook for 4–6 minutes on High/850watts/100%. Remove from the microwave, wrap in foil and stand for 5 minutes before cutting into 1.5cm ($1/2$ in)-thick slices. Allow to cool.

microwave tip 2: wash the beans, place into a freezer bag and twist the opening to close. Cook for 2–3 minutes on High/850watts/100%.

crisp bean & pea salad

serves: 6-8 prep: 15 mins cooking: 5 mins

	Pinch of salt
200g	(1 cup) green beans, topped
200g	(1 cup) butter beans, topped
1	bunch snake beans, ends trimmed, cut into 10cm lengths
150g	snow peas, topped
150g	sugar snap peas, topped

balsamic honey dressing

80mls	($1/3$ cup) extra virgin olive oil
5 tsp	balsamic vinegar
1 tsp	Dijon mustard
2 tsp	honey
	Salt & ground black pepper, to taste

1 To make the dressing, combine the extra virgin olive oil, balsamic vinegar, mustard, honey and salt and pepper in a screw-top jar and shake well.

2 Bring a large saucepan of water to the boil. Add the salt, green beans, butter beans and snake beans and bring back to the boil. Boil for 1–2 minutes or until the beans are tender crisp. Use a slotted spoon to transfer the beans to a colander and then refresh them under cold running water. Drain well.

3 Add the snow peas and sugar snap peas to the saucepan and bring back to the boil. Boil for 30 seconds or until the peas are tender crisp and bright green. Drain and refresh under cold running water.

4 To serve, combine vegetables in a bowl and toss through the dressing.

easy fried rice

serves: 4 prep: 10 mins cooking: 5–6 mins

2 tbs	peanut oil
150g	(5 oz) rindless bacon rashers
200g	(about 20) small green prawns, peeled
3	eggs, lightly whisked
640g	(4 cups) cooked long-grain rice
1	small red capsicum (pepper), deseeded, diced
300g	fresh peas, shelled
80g	(1 cup) bean sprouts
1¹/₂ tbs	light soy sauce
2	green shallots, thinly sliced

1 Heat the peanut oil in a large wok over high heat. Add the bacon and prawns, and stir-fry for 1 minute.

2 Reduce the heat to medium-high, pour the whisked eggs into the wok and stir with a wooden spoon to break the eggs up until just set.

3 Add the cooked rice, capsicum and peas and cook, tossing, for 1–2 minutes or until well combined.

4 Add the bean sprouts and soy sauce and cook for 1 minute or until combined and heated through. Serve sprinkled with the green shallots.

marinated fish with warm chickpea & tomato salad

serves: 4   prep: 20 mins (plus 30 mins marinating time)   cooking: 30 mins

4   (about 175g or 6 oz each) fish fillets (like blue eye (trevalla), snapper or morwong (sea bream)
4   egg tomatoes, quartered
1   red onion, quartered
2   300g (10 oz) cans chickpeas, rinsed, drained
60mls   (1/4 cup) extra virgin olive oil
2 tbs   fresh lemon juice
1   garlic clove, finely chopped
2 tbs   chopped fresh coriander
    Salt & ground black pepper, to taste

spiced yoghurt marinade

60g   (1/4 cup) natural yoghurt
2 tbs   fresh lemon juice
1   garlic clove, finely chopped
1/2 tsp   ground cumin
1/2 tsp   ground coriander

1 Preheat oven to 200°C (400°F). Cover a baking tray with non-stick baking paper.
2 To make the marinade, place yoghurt, lemon juice, garlic, cumin and coriander in a small bowl and stir to combine.
3 Place the fish fillets into a large glass or ceramic dish. Pour the marinade over and turn the fish to coat in the marinade. Cover and place in the fridge for 30 minutes, or overnight if time permits, to marinate.
4 Place the tomatoes and onion on the lined tray. Roast in preheated oven for 20 minutes or until just starting to brown. Remove the tomatoes from the oven. Leave the oven on.
5 Combine the roasted tomatoes, onion, chickpeas, olive oil, lemon juice, garlic and coriander in a medium bowl. Season with salt and pepper and mix well. Set aside and keep warm.
6 Drain the fish fillets and arrange on the lined baking tray. Cook in preheated oven for 8-10 minutes or until fish is just cooked through and it flakes when tested with a fork. (See microwave tip.) Serve the fish with the warm chickpea salad.

microwave tip: drain the fish fillets and arrange in a single layer on a microwave-safe plate or fish steamer. Cover loosely with damp paper towel and cook for 6-8 minutes on Medium/500watts/50% or until just cooked through.

This irresistible relish is delicious served with wood-fired bread or as an accompaniment to barbecued lamb or chicken. Or try it tossed through your favourite pasta.

eggplant & olive relish

makes: about 2 cups   prep: 10 mins (plus 20 mins degorging and cooling time)   cooking: 30 mins

2	medium (about 700g) eggplant
	Salt, for degorging
125mls	(1/2 cup) olive oil
1	medium red capsicum (pepper), quartered deseeded, coarsely chopped
2	garlic cloves, finely chopped
55g	(1/3 cup) kalamata olives, pitted, coarsely chopped
2 tbs	fresh oregano leaves
	Fresh oregano sprigs (optional), to garnish

1 Coarsely chop the eggplant and sprinkle lightly with salt. Place in a colander and allow to stand for 10 minutes. Rinse the eggplant well under cold running water. Drain and pat dry with paper towel.

2 Heat the olive oil in a large saucepan over medium-high heat. Add eggplant, capsicum and garlic and stir to coat with the olive oil. Reduce heat to medium-low, cover and cook, stirring occasionally, for 30 minutes or until the eggplant has softened and the mixture is thick.

3 Transfer the relish to a heat-resistant bowl. Stand for 10 minutes to cool slightly.

4 Stir in the olives and oregano and serve warm or at room temperature, garnished with the oregano sprigs, if desired.

Believe it or not, these scrumptious tarts are low-fat. They work just as well if you use plums or peaches instead of nectarines, and currants instead of raisins.

nectarine banana & muscatel raisin tarts

serves: 4   prep: 20 mins   cooking: 15–20 mins

2	small bananas
2	ripe nectarines, washed
1	lime, juiced
40g	(¹/₄ cup) muscatel raisins
1 tbs	maple syrup
80mls	(¹/₃ cup) grape juice
6	sheets filo pastry
1 tbs	almond or hazelnut meal
	Extra light olive oil spray
200g	low-fat yoghurt, to serve

1 Preheat oven to 180°C (350°F). Line a baking tray with non-stick baking paper.

2 Peel the bananas and diagonally cut each into 4 pieces. Cut nectarines in half, remove the stones and then cut each half into 3 wedges. Place the bananas and nectarines into a bowl. Drizzle with the lime juice. (This adds flavour and prevents the bananas from browning.)

3 Combine the raisins, maple syrup and grape juice in a small saucepan. Bring to the boil and then simmer, uncovered, over medium-low heat for 5 minutes or until juice is reduced to a thick, syrupy consistency.

4 Lay the filo sheets flat on a cutting board and, working quickly so the pastry doesn't dry out, use a saucer as a guide to cut two 17cm (7 in) circles through all the layers. Place 4 separate filo circles on the lined baking tray and sprinkle each with 1 tsp of the almond or hazelnut meal. Cover each with 2 more circles of filo and lightly spray the edge of each with the olive oil spray. Roll about 3cm (1 in) of the edge of each filo circle towards the centre three times with damp fingertips, pressing firmly, to create a border.

5 Arrange 2 banana pieces and 3 wedges of nectarine on each filo circle. Divide the raisins among the tarts and then spoon the raisin syrup over (about 1 tsp over each).

6 Bake in preheated oven for 15–20 minutes or until the pastry is golden. Serve warm with the yoghurt.

Homemade ice-blocks could always be found in our freezer when I was growing up, usually made from brightly coloured cordial (red was the favourite). These fruit pops, based on summer fruit purees, are for grown-ups too.

fresh fruit pops

makes: 12   prep: 20 mins (plus 3–4 hours freezing time)

250g (1²/₃ cups, 1 punnet) strawberries, hulled

250g (1²/₃ cups) peeled and deseeded watermelon flesh

250g (1²/₃ cups) peeled and deseeded honeydew melon flesh

1 large mango, peeled, flesh chopped

12 Paddle-pop moulds or 12 plastic cups and 12 wooden Paddle-pop sticks

1 Puree the fruits separately in a food processor or blender until smooth.

2 Pour each puree into 3 paddle-pop moulds or plastic cups.

3 If using Paddle-pop moulds, cover with the tops and freeze for 3–4 hours or until set. If using the plastic cups, freeze for 1 hour or until set enough to support a Paddle-pop stick. Then place a wooden Paddle-pop stick into the centre of each fruit pop and refreeze for 2–3 hours or until set. Remove the fruit pops from the moulds or cups to serve.

variations

■ add 2 tbs natural low-fat yoghurt to 250mls (1 cup) watermelon puree for a refreshing alternative. Also add yoghurt to mango, berry, rockmelon and peach purees.

■ try mixing fruit purees: pineapple and mango or strawberry and raspberry, and flavouring them with a little citrus juice like mango with orange juice or honeydew melon with lime juice.

MELONS

■ Choose melons that are heavy for their size, then apply the smell/sniff test. A pleasant, fruit aroma typical of that particular melon is always a good indication of flavour.

■ To make a granita: puree deseeded watermelon flesh in a food processor or blender until smooth. Pass it through a sieve and then sweeten the watermelon juice with caster sugar. Freeze in an airtight container until partially set. Scrape it with a fork to break up the ice crystals. Return it to the freezer until it sets. Scrape it with a fork again before serving topped with mixed fresh berries in glasses.

■ Make a fruit salad with chunks of honeydew melon, watermelon and rockmelon, toss with lots of fresh mint and serve well chilled.

good melon partners: ginger, honey, sugar, berries, prosciutto, brown sugar, mint.

mango & nectarine compote

serves: 8 prep: 15 mins (plus 15 mins cooling & overnight chilling time) cooking: 5 mins

550g   (2^1/$_2$ cups) sugar
750mls (3 cups) sparkling white wine
60mls   (^{1}/$_4$ cup) fresh lime juice
1   vanilla bean pod, halved (optional)
4   mangoes, peeled, flesh sliced
4   nectarines, quartered, stones removed
        Thick cream or vanilla ice-cream, to serve

1 Combine the sugar, sparkling white wine, lime juice and vanilla bean, if using, in a medium saucepan. Stir over medium heat until sugar dissolves. Bring to the boil then remove from heat and cool for 15 minutes.

2 Place mangoes and nectarines in a ceramic or glass dish and pour the warm syrup over. Cover with plastic wrap and place in the fridge overnight.

3 Serve chilled with cream or ice-cream.

Not owning an ice-cream maker can be frustrating (especially when most recipes require one). I developed this recipe specifically for those who don't have an ice-cream maker. It gives a wonderfully rich, velvety ice-cream—without all the fuss. Eat it within a month.

basic vanilla ice-cream

serves: 4–6 (makes about 1 litre)   prep: 15 mins (plus 8–10 hours freezing time)   cooking: 5–8 mins

5	egg yolks
150g	(^{2}/$_3$ cup) caster sugar
1^1/$_2$ tsp	vanilla essence
375mls	(1^1/$_2$ cups) thickened cream
125mls	(^{1}/$_2$ cup) milk

variations

■ **very berry ice-cream:** leave out the milk. Combine 500g (2 punnets) strawberries, hulled and chopped, and 125g (1 punnet) raspberries with 2 tbs of the caster sugar and set aside for 20 minutes. Roughly mash the berry mixture and then strain off any juice into a small saucepan (you will have about 80mls/^{1}/$_3$ cup of juice). Reserve the flesh. Simmer the juice until reduced by about half. Cool. Continue as in the basic recipe with the remaining 110g (^{1}/$_2$ cup) caster sugar and stir the reduced fruit juice and berry flesh into the egg yolk mixture before folding in the cream. Freeze. Serves 6 (makes about 1 litre).

■ **rich chocolate ice-cream:** reduce egg yolks to 4. Reduce the caster sugar to 75g (^{1}/$_3$ cup). Bring the milk just to a simmer in a saucepan and pour it over 200g (7 oz) chopped, good-quality dark chocolate in a heat-resistant bowl. Stand for 1 minute and then stir until smooth and well combined. Continue as in the basic recipe and stir the chocolate mixture into the egg yolk mixture before folding in the cream. Freeze. Serves 6–8 (makes about 1 litre).

■ **espresso ice-cream:** increase the milk to 250mls (1 cup). Heat the milk with 110g (^{3}/$_4$ cup) espresso coffee beans, roughly crushed, in a saucepan over low heat until simmering. Remove from heat and cool to room temperature. Strain through a fine sieve. Continue as in the basic recipe and stir the coffee milk into the egg yolk mixture before folding in the cream. Freeze. Serves 6 (makes about 1 litre).

1 Combine egg yolks and caster sugar in a heat-resistant bowl. Place over a saucepan of simmering water and use a wire whisk or electric hand beaters to whisk constantly for 5–8 minutes or until the mixture is thick and pale and a ribbon trail forms when the whisk or beaters are lifted.

2 Remove the mixture from the heat, add the vanilla essence and whisk until cooled to room temperature. (The mixture will thicken even further as it cools.)

3 Use a hand whisk or electric beaters to whisk the cream in a medium mixing bowl until soft peaks form.

4 Stir the milk into the egg yolk mixture until well combined. Then use a large metal spoon or spatula to fold half the whipped cream into the mixture until almost combined. Add the remaining cream and fold very gently until thoroughly combined.

5 Pour the ice-cream mixture into an airtight container and seal. Place in the freezer and freeze for 8–10 hours or until firm.

6 Transfer the ice-cream to the fridge 20 minutes before serving to soften slightly and evenly.

rich chocolate truffles

makes: about 30   prep: 25 mins (plus 4 hours chilling time)   cooking: 10 mins

300g   (10 oz) good-quality dark
        chocolate, chopped
80mls   (¹/₃ cup) thickened (whipped) cream
2 tbs   freshly brewed strong coffee
100g   (1 cup) cocoa powder

1 Place the chocolate, cream and coffee in a medium heat-resistant bowl or in the top of a double saucepan and stir over simmering water until the mixture is smooth. (See microwave tip).

2 Transfer the mixture to another bowl and place in the fridge to chill for 3 hours or until firm enough to roll into balls.

3 Line a tray with non-stick baking paper. Sift the cocoa onto a plate or into a shallow cake pan.

4 Use your hands dusted with cocoa powder to quickly roll a small spoonful of the chocolate mixture into a ball about 2-3cm (1 in) in diameter and drop it into the cocoa powder. Repeat, rolling about 5 more balls, then roll the balls in the cocoa until well coated. Place the truffles on the lined tray. Repeat with the remaining chocolate mixture and cocoa.

5 Place the truffles in the fridge for at least 1 hour before serving. Keep in an airtight container lined with grease-proof paper for up to 2 weeks or freeze for up to 1 month.

microwave tip: place the chocolate, cream and coffee in a medium heat-resistant, microwave-safe bowl and heat, uncovered, for 1–2 minutes on Medium-High/650watts/70%, stirring every minute, or until the chocolate is melted and the mixture is smooth.

BERRIES

■ For the ultimate sweet snack, serve a large platter of ripe strawberries, still with their hulls, alongside a bowl of dark brown sugar and crème fraîche or sour cream. Dunk the strawberries into the cream and then into the brown sugar.

■ Sprinkle a mixture of raspberries and hulled strawberries with a little balsamic vinegar and brown sugar. Toss and let macerate for a little while before serving with thick cream or over vanilla ice-cream.

■ To make Janelle Bloom's (agt's microwave consultant) strawberry jam: hull and then halve 500g (2 cups) strawberries. Place them with 60mls (¹/₄ cup) fresh lemon juice and finely grated rind of 1 lemon in a large heatproof, microwave-safe bowl. Cover and cook for 4 minutes on High/850watts/100%. Remove the cover and stir in 440g (2 cups) sugar. Cook, uncovered, for 20–25 minutes on High/850watts/100% or until the jam sets when tested (see the nectarine and brandy jam recipe on p 99). Ladle into hot sterilised jars and seal. Makes about 500mls (2 cups).

good berry partners: vanilla ice-cream, orange juice, brown sugar, sponge cake, lemon, mint, balsamic vinegar, orange liqueur, mascarpone, cream, sour cream, passionfruit, sparkling wine.

strawberries with orange syrup & ice-cream

serves: 4 prep: 5 mins (plus 3–5 mins standing time) cooking: 2–3 mins

2	oranges, juiced
1¹/₂ tbs	brown sugar
250g	(1 punnet) small strawberries, hulled
	Vanilla ice-cream, to serve
	Savoiardi (sponge finger) biscuits, to serve

1 Combine the orange juice and brown sugar in a small saucepan and stir over high heat until the sugar dissolves. Bring to the boil and then remove the saucepan from the heat. (See microwave tip.)

2 Add the strawberries to the syrup and stand for 3–5 minutes.

3 Serve with the ice-cream accompanied by the savoiardi biscuits.

microwave tip: combine the orange juice and brown sugar in a small microwave-safe bowl. Cover with a lid or plastic wrap and cook for 2-3 minutes on High/850watts/100%. Carefully remove the cover and stir to ensure the sugar has dissolved.

spiced cherries
with goat's cheese cream

serves: 6   prep: 20–30 mins (plus 6 hours standing time)   cooking: 15 mins

2	lemons
500mls	(2 cups) water
220g	(1 cup) caster sugar
8	whole cloves
2	cinnamon sticks
80mls	(1/3 cup) dessert wine or port (optional)
1kg	cherries, stems left intact (if desired)

goat's cheese cream

300g	goat's cheese
200mls	thickened (whipped) cream
250g	(1 cup) Greek-style natural yoghurt
55g	(1/4 cup) caster sugar

1 To make the goat's cheese cream, line a sieve with a piece of muslin, or a clean, loosely woven tea towel. Place the goat's cheese in a bowl and use a fork to mash thoroughly. Add the cream, yoghurt and sugar and use a wooden spoon to beat until combined and smooth. Spoon the mixture into the lined sieve, cover the mixture with the overhanging cloth and place the sieve over a bowl. Place in the fridge for at least 6 hours to drain.

2 Meanwhile, peel the rind from the lemons using a vegetable peeler. Remove the white pith from the rind and cut the rind into thin strips. Juice the fruit.

3 Combine the lemon juice, water and caster sugar in a large saucepan and stir over low heat until sugar dissolves. Add the lemon rind strips, cloves and cinnamon sticks and bring to the boil. Reduce heat to medium and simmer, uncovered, for 10 minutes. (See microwave tip.)

4 Remove syrup from heat, strain liquid into a heat-resistant bowl and cool to room temperature. Discard the spices. Stir in the dessert wine or port, if using.

5 Add the cherries, cover and place in the fridge for at least 3 hours or overnight, if time permits, to macerate.

6 To serve, spoon the goat's cheese cream into serving dishes and top with the spiced cherries.

microwave tip: combine the lemon juice, water and caster sugar in a medium heat-resistant, microwave-safe bowl. Heat, uncovered, for 2–3 minutes on High/ 850watts/100%. Stir to dissolve the sugar. Add the lemon rind strips, cloves and cinnamon sticks and cook, uncovered, for 1 minute on High/850watts/100%. Then cook for 4–5 minutes on Medium-High/650watts/70% or until the syrup thickens slightly.

Cherries and goat's cheese make lovely partners. If you don't particularly like the distinctive flavour of goat's cheese simply replace it with fresh ricotta.

peaches basted with honey & wine

serves: 6   prep: 5 mins   cooking: 35 mins

6	medium, firm, ripe peaches, washed
250mls	(1 cup) white wine (like riesling)
125mls	(¹/₂ cup) water
1	cinnamon stick
1 tsp	vanilla essence
125mls	(¹/₂ cup) honey
	Thick (whipped) cream or vanilla ice-cream, to serve

1 Preheat oven to 170°C (330°F).

2 Place whole peaches into a 20 x 30cm (8 x 11 in) shallow oven-proof dish.

3 Combine the wine, water, cinnamon stick and vanilla essence in a jug and pour over the peaches. Then drizzle evenly with the honey.

4 Bake in preheated oven for 35 minutes, basting with the liquid every 10 minutes, or until the peaches are tender.

5 Serve peaches and their liquid warm or at room temperature with cream or ice-cream.

These simple poached plums have been enhanced with cardamom—
a spice with a warm, bittersweet, refreshing flavour. When buying
cardamom pods look for the green ones that have a more intense
flavour than the other varieties. It is best to crush them lightly with
the blade of a knife to split the pod and expose the tiny black seeds
before using them so you can make the most of their flavour.

poached cardamom plums

serves: 4   prep: 10 mins   cooking: 14-18 mins

250mls	(1 cup) water
110g	($^1/_2$ cup) caster sugar
5	cardamom pods, lightly crushed
8	plums (variety of your choice), halved, stones removed
2	200g (7 oz) cartons natural yoghurt, to serve

1 Combine the water, caster sugar and cardamom pods in a medium, heavy-based saucepan and stir over a medium-low heat until the sugar dissolves completely. Bring to the boil and simmer, uncovered, for 8–10 minutes or until the mixture is slightly syrupy.

2 Add the plums, cover and simmer for 4–5 minutes or until the plums are just tender. (See microwave tip.)

3 Serve warm or chilled with the yoghurt.

microwave tip: combine the water, caster sugar and cardamom pods in a large heat resistant microwave-safe bowl. Cook, uncovered, stirring every minute, for 4–5 minutes on High/850watts/100%. Add the plums, cover and cook for 2–3 minutes on Medium/500watts/50% or until the plums are just tender.

Summer is a great time for making jam—berries, plums, peaches and nectarines all make fabulous spreads. This jam will keep in a cool dark cupboard for up to a year. Once you've opened it, pop it in the fridge where it should keep for another few months.

nectarine & brandy jam

makes: about 1 litre (4 cups)   prep: 20 mins (plus 10 mins standing time)   cooking: 1 1/4 hours

2kg	(about 12) nectarines
880g	(4 cups) caster sugar
250mls	(1 cup) water
125mls	(1/2 cup) brandy
5 tbs	fresh lemon juice

1 Cut a shallow cross into the base of each nectarine then plunge them into a large saucepan of boiling water for 30 seconds. Drain and refresh under cold running water. Drain. Use a sharp knife to peel away the skin then cut around the stones to remove the flesh. Cut the nectarine flesh into thin slices.

2 Combine the caster sugar, water, brandy and lemon juice in a large saucepan and stir over low heat until the sugar dissolves.

3 Add the nectarine slices and bring to a gentle boil over medium heat. Simmer, for 75 minutes or until jam reaches setting point (105°C or 220°F on sugar thermometer). To test, place a teaspoon of jam on a cold saucer in the freezer for 2 minutes or until cooled to room temperature. Run a finger through the jam—if the surface wrinkles and the jam remains in two separate portions, it is ready.

4 Remove the jam from heat and stand for 10 minutes. Use a large spoon to skim any scum from the surface of the jam. Ladle the jam into hot sterilised jars (see note below). Seal and invert jars for 2 minutes. Turn jars upright and allow to cool. Label and store in a cool cupboard.

note: to sterilise jars, wash the jars and lids in warm soapy water and rinse well. Place them in a large saucepan and cover with water. Bring to the boil and boil for 10 minutes. Transfer jars and lids to a baking tray lined with baking paper or newspaper and place in an oven preheated to 100°C (212°F) until dry. (If using screw-top lids or rubber gaskets don't put these in the oven—just air-dry them in a colander after boiling them.) Use the jars and lids straight from the oven.

autumn
a season of transformation & reflection

The fresh produce of summer is replaced by fruit and vegetables that reflect the hues of the turning leaves. The vibrant oranges and reds, earthy yellows and browns and warming mauves of quinces, pomegranates, apples, mandarins, root vegetables, figs, pears, pumpkins and chestnuts mirror the season. They define this time of year.

Autumn guides you when it comes to cooking the produce it offers. Just as we fossick in our wardrobes and add more layers of clothing through the season, so our meals and cooking techniques become more involved as the weather turns.

There's nothing like a cool change to get you to turn on your oven. It doesn't matter whether it's to bake a batch of biscuits or a

pie, to cook a pudding or to roast vegetables: the oven not only warms the house, it has the ability to transform food. Layers of buttered bread soaked in milk and eggs become a warm and delicious dessert, a pleasure to devour (see p 150 for our Easter version). Ugly root vegetables sweeten and take on a golden colour to make pleasing partners for roasted meats (see p 122). And the pungent flesh of whole heads of garlic softens and mellows to a point where you can eat it by the spoonful (see p 110).

In autumn we also begin to think about leaving things on the stove top a little longer: like slow simmering curries, meatballs poached in a tomato sauce (see p 131) and large pots of communal soup. Pumpkin soup—perhaps seasoned with nutmeg, a little cumin or even some Thai red curry paste—is an old favourite. Pumpkin, like cultivated mushrooms and potatoes, is available all year, but is rediscovered every autumn.

Limes, on the other hand, are seasonal and will never be cheaper than in autumn. Now is the time to transform them into something to be enjoyed throughout the year: for example simmering, punchy chutney (see p 133).

Autumn is all the excuse I need to head for the kitchen, switch on the oven, and fill the house with the warmth of baking. I watch as biscuit doughs spread and sweet muffin mixtures rise. It is the promise of eating those biscuits or muffins warm with a steaming cuppa that is the greatest pleasure of all.

autumn's best
a guide to help you use produce at the height of its season

vegetables

- Asian greens:
  bok choy
  choy sum
  gai lum
  Chinese water spinach [on choy]
  Chinese cabbage (wong nga bok)
- beans:
  borlotti (early)
  green
  Italian flat (early))
  snake (early to mid)
- broccoli (mid to late)
- brussels sprouts (mid to late)
- cabbage
- capsicum (peppers) (early)
- carrots
- cauliflower (late)
- celeriac (celery root) (late)
- chestnuts (mid to late)
- chillies
- corn
- cucumber (early to mid)
- eggplant
- garlic
- ginger
- kohlrabi (late)

- leeks (late)
- lettuce
- mushrooms (cultivated)
- okra (early)
- onions:
  brown
  green shallots/green onions/
  scallions
  French shallots/eschallots
  red/Spanish
  spring
  white
- parsnip (mid to late)
- peas:
  green (early)
  sugar snap (late)
- potatoes (general)

- pumpkin
- silverbeet (late)
- spinach/English
  spinach
- swede
- sweet potato
- squash
- tomatoes
- turnip (late)
- witlof (chicory)
- zucchini (mid to late)

This information may vary slightly depending on where you live and/or weather conditions

fruit

- apples
  bonza (late)
  braeburn (late)
  fuji (mid to late)
  golden delicious
  granny smith (late)
  jonathan
  pink lady (late)
  red delicious (mid to late)
  royal gala
- avocados
- bananas
- berries:
  blackberries (early)
  raspberries (early)
  strawberries
- carambola (star fruit)
- figs (early to mid)

- grapefruit
  yellow (mid to late)
- grapes
- guava
- kiwifruit
- lemons (mid to late)
- limes (early to mid)
- mandarins (mid to late)
- melons:
  honeydew (early)
  rockmelon (cantaloupe)
  (early)
  watermelon (early)
- nashi (mid to late)
- oranges:
  navel (late)
  valencia (early to mid)
- papaya (early to mid)

- passionfruit
- peaches (early)
- pears:
  beurre bosc (mid to late)
  josephine
  packham (late)
  williams (early to mid)
- persimmons (mid)
- plums (early to mid)
- pomegranates (mid to late)
- pomelos (late)
- quince (mid to late)
- rambutans (early to mid)
- tamarillos (mid)

classic chicken soup

serves: 6 prep: 30 mins (plus overnight chilling time) cooking: 1 hour

1	1.4kg (size 14) chicken
2	large brown onions, finely chopped
2 cups	loosely packed fresh continental parsley leaves
4	garlic cloves, crushed
60mls	($^1/_4$ cup) fresh lemon juice
2 tbs	soy sauce
5	celery sticks, cut into 1cm pieces
5	medium carrots, cut into 1cm pieces
2	medium tomatoes, halved
1.5L	(6 cups) water
	Salt & ground black pepper, to taste

1 Rinse the inside of the chicken. Remove the tail and neck, and as much skin as possible.

2 Combine the onions, parsley, garlic, lemon juice and soy sauce in a large saucepan. Cook over medium heat for 5–8 minutes or until onions are soft. Add chicken, celery, carrots, tomatoes and water and bring to the boil. Reduce heat to low and simmer, covered, for 1 hour or until the chicken is tender and comes away from the bones easily.

3 Remove from heat, cool for 10 minutes and place in the fridge to chill overnight. (This allows the fat to rise and set on the surface.)

4 Next day, remove the soup from the fridge and use a large metal spoon to remove the layer of solidified fat from the surface of the stock.

5 Remove the chicken from the soup and place in a large bowl. Use your fingers to remove the meat from the bones and shred into pieces. Discard the bones. Return the chicken meat to the soup.

6 Bring the soup to the boil over medium heat and simmer until the chicken and vegetables are heated through. Remove the soup from the heat and skim a piece of paper towel over the surface to absorb any excess fat from the surface. Season with salt and pepper and ladle the soup into deep soup bowls. Sprinkle with a little extra pepper and serve.

pear parmesan & rocket salad

serves: 4 as an entree or accompaniment   prep: 15 mins

50g	(1/2 bunch) rocket, trimmed
1/2	small green oakleaf lettuce, leaves separated, washed, dried
50g	(21/2 tbs) piece parmesan, shaved
60g	(1/2 cup) walnuts
2 tbs	chopped fresh chives
1	(about 300g) pear (like beurre bosc, packham or williams)

cider dressing

2 tbs	olive oil
1 tbs	cider vinegar
	Salt & ground black pepper, to taste

1 To make the dressing, place the olive oil and vinegar in a small bowl. Season with salt and pepper and whisk to combine.

2 Place the rocket, lettuce, parmesan, walnuts and chives in a large bowl.

3 Peel, quarter and core the pear. Slice each quarter into four. Add to the salad with the dressing and toss well. Serve immediately.

When roasted, garlic takes on a soft texture with a subtle, nutty, sweet flavour. Try it spread on toasted, Italian-style bread like ciabatta and topped with sliced tomato or added to mashed potato, pasta, casseroles or butter to top baked potatoes. The garlic flesh removed from the cloves will store in an airtight container in the fridge for up to a week.

roasted garlic with rosemary

serves: 4 prep: 5 mins (plus 10 mins standing time) cooking: 55 mins

4	whole garlic bulbs
4	sprigs fresh rosemary, leaves picked
2 tbs	olive oil
1 tbs	fresh lemon juice
	Salt & ground black pepper, to taste

1 Preheat oven to 200°C (400°F).

2 Cut about 1cm from the top of each garlic bulb to expose the individual garlic cloves. Discard the tops. Place the garlic bulbs in a small ovenproof dish. Sprinkle the rosemary leaves over the bulbs and then drizzle with the olive oil and lemon juice. Season with salt and pepper.

3 Cover the dish with foil and bake in preheated oven for 55 minutes or until the garlic is very soft when tested with a skewer.

4 Remove the garlic from oven and stand, covered, for 10 minutes.

5 Serve the roasted garlic straight from the bulb or squeeze it from the cloves and use as desired.

Laksa, the spicy, aromatic soup from Malaysia, is a meal in itself. This homemade curry paste will keep in an airtight container in the fridge for up to 2 weeks. If time is short you can use 2–3 tbs of your favourite bought red curry paste.

prawn laksa

serves: 4 as a main   prep: 25 mins   cooking: 30–35 mins

500g	(1 pound) green prawns
1½ tbs	vegetable oil
500mls	(2 cups) water
200g	cellophane (mung bean) noodles
180g	(²/₃ cup) tofu (optional), cut in thin slices and then in 3cm (1 in) squares
375mls	(1½ cups) fish or vegetable stock
1	400ml (2 cups) can coconut milk
250g	bean sprouts
⅓ cup	chopped fresh coriander leaves
4	green shallots, sliced, to serve Fresh coriander leaves, extra, to garnish

curry paste

1	medium brown onion, chopped
2	garlic cloves, crushed
3cm	(1 in) piece fresh ginger, peeled, grated
2	lemon grass stalks, pale section only, sliced
8	macadamia nuts
1 tsp	shrimp paste
1 tbs	fish sauce, or to taste
1 tbs	sambal oelek
1 tbs	fresh lemon juice
1 tsp	ground cumin
1 tsp	ground coriander

1 To make curry paste, place all the ingredients in the bowl of a food processor and process until smooth and well combined. Set aside.

2 Peel and devein the prawns leaving the tails intact. Reserve the heads and shells.

3 Heat 2 tsp of the vegetable oil in a large saucepan over medium heat and cook the reserved prawn heads and shells for 5 minutes or until they change colour and become aromatic. Add the water and bring to the boil. Reduce heat to medium and simmer, uncovered, for 10 minutes or until the liquid is reduced by half. Strain the stock and discard the solids. Reserve the prawn stock.

4 Cook the cellophane noodles in a large saucepan of boiling water for 2 minutes. Drain and reserve.

5 Heat the remaining vegetable oil in a large saucepan over medium heat and cook the tofu, if using, turning occasionally, until lightly golden. Remove the tofu from the pan and set aside.

6 Add the reserved prawn stock, fish or vegetable stock and reserved curry paste to the saucepan and bring to the boil. Reduce heat to low, stir in the coconut milk, reserved peeled prawns and the fried tofu and simmer gently for 3–5 minutes or until the prawns change colour and are just cooked. (It is important that you simmer the soup gently at this point as the coconut milk may separate if boiled.) Stir in the chopped coriander.

7 To serve, rinse the noodles under hot water to reheat. Drain and divide them among four deep serving bowls. Ladle the soup over and top with the bean sprouts. Garnish with the green shallots and the coriander leaves.

This soup is quick to whip up. For a tasty variation shred 2 poached

chicken breast fillets and add to the soup with the stock.

The cumin croutons are also fabulous served with tomato soup.

creamy corn soup with cumin croutons

serves: 4 as an entree   prep: 10 mins   cooking: 8–10 mins

2	thick slices bread, crusts removed
	Light olive oil spray
1/2 tsp	cumin seeds
1 tbs	olive oil
1	medium brown onion, finely chopped
2	420g (12 oz) cans creamed corn
410mls	(1²/₃ cup) vegetable or chicken stock

1 Preheat oven to 180°C (350°F).

2 Lightly spray each of the bread slices on one side with the olive oil spray. Sprinkle evenly with the cumin seeds and then press them into the bread. Cut each slice into 4 squares. Cut each square in half to make triangles. (You will end up with 16 triangles.) Place on a baking tray and bake in preheated oven for 5–7 minutes or until golden.

3 Meanwhile, heat the olive oil in a large saucepan over medium heat. Add the onion and cook, stirring occasionally, for 5 minutes or until soft.

4 Add the creamed corn and stock. Cook over medium-low heat, stirring occasionally, for 4–5 minutes or until heated through. (See microwave tip.)

5 Serve the soup with the cumin croutons.

microwave tip: combine the oil and onion in medium, heat-resistant, microwave-safe bowl and cook, uncovered, for 3–4 minutes on Medium/500watts/50% or until soft. Stir in creamed corn and stock. Heat for 3–4 minutes on Medium/500watts/50% or until heated through.

Pears and pork are well suited, especially when the pears are roasted with honey and butter until they become sticky enough to melt in your mouth. Serve this dish with steamed sliced zucchini and boiled waxy potatoes tossed in a little butter.

pork with honey roasted pears

serves: 4 prep: 20 mins cooking: 30 mins

2	(about 250-300g or 85-100 oz each) just-ripe pears (like beurre bosc, packham or williams)
2 tbs	honey
60g	(3 tbs) butter
1 tbs	olive oil
4	(about 150g or 50 oz each) pork fillets
	Salt & ground black pepper, to taste

1 Preheat oven to 220°C (424°F).

2 Peel, quarter and core pears. Cut each quarter in half lengthways. Place in a large bowl.

3 Combine 1 tbs honey and 20g (1 tbs) of the butter in a small saucepan and cook over low heat until the butter is melted. Pour over the pears and toss to coat well.

4 Transfer pears and any liquid to a large non-stick roasting pan. Roast in preheated oven for 15–20 minutes or until tender when tested with a skewer.

5 Meanwhile, heat the olive oil and half the remaining butter in a large frying pan over medium-high heat until the butter bubbles. Add the pork, season with salt and pepper and cook for 5 minutes or until browned on all sides. Remove from pan.

6 Reduce oven temperature to 200°C (400°F). Add the pork fillets to the baking dish with the pears and cook for a further 6–8 minutes or until the pork is just cooked through.

7 Remove from the oven and cut the pork diagonally into thick slices. Divide the pork between serving plates. Add the remaining honey and butter to the pears and stir to combine. Spoon the pears and juices over the pork. Serve immediately.

tofu pumpkin
& bean stir-fry
with basil

serves: 4 prep: 20 mins cooking: 20 mins

1 tbs	salt-reduced soy sauce
2 tsp	fish sauce
1 tsp	sesame oil
2	garlic cloves, finely chopped
300g	(10 oz) firm tofu, drained, cut into 2cm (1 in) pieces
1kg	(2.2 pounds) piece pumpkin, peeled, deseeded, cut into 2cm pieces
2 tbs	peanut or vegetable oil
250g	(1²/₃ cups) green beans, topped, halved
3 tsp	sambal oelek, or to taste
2 tbs	water
1	bunch English spinach, washed
¹/₂	bunch fresh basil, leaves picked
100g	(²/₃ cup) unsalted, roasted peanuts or cashews, roughly chopped
	Cooked jasmine rice, to serve

1 Combine the soy sauce, fish sauce, sesame oil and garlic in a medium bowl. Add the tofu and stir gently to coat the tofu in the marinade. Set aside to marinate while preparing the other ingredients.

2 Meanwhile, steam the pumpkin over boiling water for 8 minutes or until just tender. Drain well.

3 Drain the tofu and reserve marinade. Heat a wok over high heat for 1 minute. Add 1 tbs of the oil and heat for 30–60 seconds or until hot. Add the tofu and stir-fry, gently tossing, for 2 minutes or until lightly browned. Remove from the wok with a slotted spoon and transfer to a plate. Set aside.

4 Add the remaining oil to the wok and heat over high heat for 30–60 seconds or until hot. Add the beans and stir-fry for 2 minutes. Add the pumpkin, and stir-fry, gently tossing, for 1 minute.

5 Add the sambal oelek and water to the reserved marinade. Return the tofu to the wok with the English spinach and reserved marinade mixture. Toss gently and cook until the spinach is wilted.

6 Remove from heat, add the basil and half the peanuts or cashews and toss gently to combine. Serve sprinkled with the remaining peanuts or cashews, and accompanied by the jasmine rice.

coconut chicken salad

serves: 4 as a light lunch or entree   prep: 30 mins (plus 1 hour cooling time)   cooking: 15 mins

2	single chicken breast fillets, trimmed
250mls	(1 cup) coconut milk
1	lemon grass stalk, pale section only, bruised, roughly chopped
2	small fresh red chillies, halved, deseeded
	Peanut or vegetable oil, for deep-frying
200g	(1^1/$_2$ cups) French shallots, peeled, thinly sliced
^{1}/$_2$	Chinese cabbage (wong nga bak)
1	medium cucumber, peeled, halved lengthways, deseeded, thinly sliced
^{1}/$_2$	red capsicum (pepper), halved, deseeded, thinly sliced
50g	(2^1/$_2$ tbs) bean sprouts
^{1}/$_2$	bunch fresh coriander, leaves picked
100g	(^{2}/$_3$ cup) roasted peanuts

lime dressing

2	limes, juiced
1 tbs	fish sauce
	Ground black pepper, to taste

1 Place the chicken fillets, coconut milk, lemon grass and chillies into a medium saucepan. Bring to a simmer over medium heat. Reduce heat to low, cover the saucepan with a lid, and simmer gently for 5 minutes. Turn the chicken fillets over and simmer, covered, for a further 2 minutes or until the chicken is just cooked through. Transfer the chicken and the liquid to a heat-resistant bowl and place it in the fridge for about 1 hour so the chicken can cool in the coconut milk.

2 Meanwhile, pour enough peanut or vegetable oil into a small saucepan to fill by about one third. Heat the oil over medium heat until hot. Add the sliced French shallots and deep-fry until golden. Drain on paper towel. Allow the oil to cool, and then strain. Reserve 100mls (^{1}/$_3$ cup) of the oil to make the lime dressing.

3 Remove and discard the dark, outside leaves and the inside core from the Chinese cabbage. Shred. Combine the cabbage, cucumber, capsicum, bean sprouts, coriander leaves and peanuts in a large bowl.

4 To make the lime dressing, whisk together the reserved peanut or vegetable oil, lime juice and fish sauce. Season with pepper.

5 Thinly slice cooled chicken across the grain. Toss the dressing through the salad and then place it into a large serving dish or individual bowls. Arrange the chicken slices on top and garnish with the French shallots.

vegetable tagine
with yellow split peas

serves: 4 prep: 15 mins cooking: 35–40 mins

2 tbs	olive oil
1	large brown onion, cut into wedges
105g	(^{1}/$_2$ cup) yellow split peas
2	garlic cloves, finely chopped
1	2cm piece fresh ginger, peeled, grated
1^1/$_2$ tsp	ground cumin
875mls	(3^1/$_2$ cups) vegetable stock
500g	(2 cups) tomatoes, chopped
1	medium (about 350g or ^{3}/$_4$ pound) orange sweet potato (kumara), peeled, halved lengthways, cut into 1cm-thick slices
1	bunch baby carrots, stems trimmed, peeled, halved if large
380g	(2 cups) couscous, to serve
^{1}/$_4$ cup	chopped fresh coriander
	Salt & ground black pepper, to taste

1 Heat half the olive oil in a large saucepan over medium heat and cook the onion for 5 minutes or until slightly softened. Remove onion from pan and set aside.

2 Heat the remaining oil in the saucepan over medium heat. Add the yellow split peas, garlic, ginger and cumin and cook for 2–3 minutes or until aromatic.

3 Add the stock and simmer over medium heat for 20 minutes.

4 Add the onion, tomatoes, sweet potato and carrots and simmer for 10 minutes or until the sweet potato is tender.

5 Meanwhile, prepare the couscous following packet directions.

6 Stir the coriander through the vegetable tagine and season to taste with salt and pepper. Serve with the couscous.

roasted root vegetables

serves: 6 as an accompaniment   prep: 10 mins   cooking: 1 hour

2   medium (about 300g) carrots, washed, dried
2   medium (about 400g) parsnips, washed, dried
2   small (about 450g) orange sweet potatoes (kumara), washed, dried
50g   (2¹/₂ tbs) butter
60mls   (¹/₄ cup) chicken stock
2 tbs   brown sugar
¹/₂ tsp   freshly grated or ground nutmeg
    Salt & ground black pepper, to taste

1 Preheat oven to 200°C (400°F).

2 Cut carrots, parsnips and sweet potatoes into chunks about 4cm (1.5 in) in length. Cut any wide pieces in half.

3 Melt butter in a 2-litre (8-cup) flameproof baking dish over medium heat. Add chicken stock, brown sugar and nutmeg and stir until the sugar dissolves. Remove from heat.

4 Add carrot and parsnip pieces to baking dish and toss well to coat in butter mixture. Roast in preheated oven for 15 minutes.

5 Add the sweet potato to the baking dish and toss to coat in the butter mixture. Roast for a further 45 minutes, turning vegetables over after 20 minutes, or until tender and golden. Season with salt and pepper. Serve warm or at room temperature.

stir-fried greens

serves: 6 as an accompaniment   prep: 5 mins   cooking: 5 mins

1 tbs	peanut oil
1¹/₂ tbs	sesame seeds
1	bunch bok choy, bases trimmed, leaves separated, washed, dried
350g	baby spinach leaves or 2 bunches English spinach, stems trimmed, washed, dried
1 tbs	soy sauce
1 tsp	sesame oil

1 Heat a wok over medium-high heat. Add the peanut oil to the wok and heat until hot. Add the sesame seeds and stir for 15–20 seconds or until the seeds begin to turn golden brown.

2 Add the bok choy and spinach to the wok and toss to coat in the oil. Cook, tossing, for 1¹/₂–2 minutes or until the leaves begin to wilt.

3 Add the soy sauce and sesame oil to the wok, toss to combine and cook until the sauce begins to bubble and the bok choy is bright green. Serve immediately.

hoi sin chicken & bok choy

serves: 4   prep: 10 mins   cooking: 12–15 mins

420g	(2 cups) long-grain white rice
60mls	(1/4 cup) peanut oil
50g	(1/3 cup) unsalted roasted peanuts
600g	(1.5 pounds) chicken tenderloins, halved lengthways
2	green shallots, diagonally sliced
2	garlic cloves, crushed
1	bunch baby bok choy, bases trimmed, leaves separated, washed, dried
80mls	(1/3 cup) water
60mls	(1/4 cup) hoi sin sauce

1 Cook the rice in a large saucepan of salted boiling water, following packet directions, for 12–15 minutes or until just tender. Drain.

2 Meanwhile, heat 1 tbs of the peanut oil in a wok or large frying pan over medium-high heat. Add the peanuts and stir for 1–2 minutes or until golden. Drain on paper towel.

3 Add 1 tbs of the remaining peanut oil to the wok or pan and heat. Add half the chicken and cook, tossing occasionally, for 2–3 minutes or until sealed. Set aside. Repeat with remaining oil and chicken.

4 Add the green shallots and garlic to the wok or pan and cook over medium-high heat for 30 seconds. Return all the chicken to the wok or pan with the bok choy, water and hoi sin sauce and cook, stirring, for 2–3 minutes or until the bok choy is wilted and bright green and the chicken is just cooked through.

5 Stir in the peanuts. Serve with the rice.

Indian lamb
potato & spinach curry

serves: 6   prep: 10–15 mins (plus 2–3 hours marinating time)   cooking: 1^1/4–1^1/2 hours

2 tsp	ground coriander
2 tsp	ground cumin
1 tsp	ground turmeric
1	200g carton natural yoghurt
1	lemon, juiced
1kg	(2.2 pounds) diced lean lamb (like forequarter)
2 tbs	vegetable oil
2	brown onions, diced
1	garlic clove, crushed
1kg	(2.2 pounds) potatoes (like desiree or nicola) peeled, cut into 2.5cm (1 in) cubes
1	410g can crushed peeled tomatoes
2 tbs	tomato paste
	Salt & ground black pepper, to taste
1 bunch	English spinach, trimmed, washed
	Cooked basmati rice and warm naan bread, to serve

1 Combine the coriander, cumin, turmeric, yoghurt and lemon juice in a large bowl. Add the lamb and mix well. Cover and place in the fridge for at least 2–3 hours, preferably overnight, to marinate.

2 Heat the vegetable oil in a large heavy-based saucepan over medium heat and cook the onions and garlic for 5 minutes or until soft.

3 Add the lamb mixture, potatoes, crushed tomatoes and tomato paste. Season with salt and pepper, stir to combine and bring to the boil. Reduce heat to medium-low and simmer gently, uncovered, for 1–1^1/$_4$ hours or until lamb is very tender.

4 Check the seasoning and adjust if necessary. Add the spinach and simmer for a further 3–5 minutes or until spinach is wilted.

5 Serve with the rice and warm naan bread.

MUSHROOMS

■ Dot the inside of mushroom flats with a little butter and sprinkle with lots of finely chopped garlic. Season with salt and pepper and drizzle with a little lemon juice. Cook under preheated hot grill for about 10 minutes or until tender. Spoon any juices over the mushrooms from time to time. Serve as an entree on a bed of baby spinach or rocket, or alongside barbecued meats.

■ Marinate 250g button mushrooms in 80mls (^{1}/$_3$ cup) olive oil, 2 tbs fresh lemon juice, 1 tbs balsamic vinegar and lots of ground black pepper for at least 4 hours. Serve at room temperature alongside barbecued chicken or lamb or as part of an antipasto with crusty bread.

good mushroom partners: olive oil, butter, parsley, thyme, marjoram, garlic, eggs, onion, risotto, pilaf, pasta, French shallots, wine, tarragon, green shallots.

This is a fast, tasty, no-fuss tuna pasta, perfect for

Sunday night dinner. I love to add about 1 tbs drained

and rinsed capers to this dish with the artichokes.

penne with
tuna & artichokes

serves: 4 prep: 10 mins cooking: 15 mins

500g	(16 oz) dried penne pasta
2 tbs	olive oil
1	medium red onion, thinly sliced
2	garlic cloves, crushed
250g	(9 oz) marinated artichoke hearts
1	425g (16 oz) can tuna (in oil), drained, flaked
1 tbs	fresh lemon juice
	Ground black pepper, to taste
1/3 cup	roughly chopped fresh continental parsley
	Ciabatta bread, sliced, to serve

1 Cook penne in a large saucepan of salted boiling water, following packet directions, until al dente. Drain, set aside and keep warm.

2 Heat the olive oil in the same saucepan over medium heat and cook the onion and garlic, stirring occasionally, for 5 minutes or until the onion is soft.

3 Quarter the artichoke hearts and then cut each in half. Add the cooked penne, artichoke hearts, tuna, lemon juice and pepper to taste to the onion mixture. Stir over medium heat, for 2–3 minutes or until heated through. (See microwave tip.)

4 Stir in the parsley. Serve with the ciabatta bread.

microwave tip: place the olive oil, onion and garlic in a medium heat-resistant microwave-safe bowl. Cook, uncovered, for 1 minute on High/850watts/100% or until soft. Stir in the cooked penne, artichokes, tuna, lemon juice and pepper to taste. Heat, uncovered, for 2–3 minutes on Medium-High/650watts/70% or until heated through.

moroccan meatballs with couscous

serves: 4 prep: 10–15 mins cooking: 10 mins

500g (16 oz) lean beef mince
50g (1 cup) fresh breadcrumbs
80mls (¹/₃ cup) milk
2 fresh red chillies, deseeded, finely chopped
1 tsp ground cumin
Salt & ground black pepper, to taste
500mls (2 cups) basic tomato sauce
185mls (³/₄ cup) beef stock
500mls (2 cups) water
2 tsp olive oil
Pinch of salt
380g (2 cups) couscous, to serve
20g (1 tbs) butter
¹/₂ bunch coriander, leaves roughly chopped

1 Place the beef mince, breadcrumbs, milk, chillies and cumin in a medium bowl and mix with your hands until thoroughly combined. Season with salt and pepper. Roll small portions of the mixture into walnut-sized balls. Set aside.

2 Combine the tomato sauce and stock in a large frying pan and bring to the boil. Reduce heat to medium-low and add the meatballs. Cover and simmer, turning the meatballs occasionally, for 5–8 minutes or until they are just cooked through.

3 Meanwhile, combine the water and olive oil in a medium saucepan and bring to the boil. Remove from heat and add the salt and then the couscous while stirring with a fork. Cover and stand for 2–3 minutes or until the water has been absorbed. Stir with a fork. Add the butter and heat over low heat, stirring with the fork occasionally, for about 3 minutes or until the butter melts and the grains are separated.

4 Stir the coriander through the meatball mixture and season to taste. Serve spooned over the couscous.

basic tomato sauce

makes: about 2 cups (500mls)
prep: 10 mins cooking: 45 mins

2 tbs olive oil
1 medium brown onion, finely chopped
2 garlic cloves, finely chopped
2 400g (12 oz) cans whole peeled tomatoes
2 tbs tomato paste
2 tsp sugar, or to taste
Salt & ground black pepper, to taste

1 Combine the olive oil, onion and garlic in a medium saucepan and cook over low heat, stirring frequently, for 12–15 minutes or until soft and translucent.

2 Add tomatoes with their liquid. Crush them into pieces with a wooden spoon against the side of the saucepan or with a potato masher. Add the tomato paste and sugar. Stir to combine.

3 Bring the sauce to the boil. Reduce heat to medium-low and simmer, uncovered, stirring frequently, for 25–30 minutes or until thick and all the watery liquid has evaporated. The best way to judge if the sauce is ready is by its flavour and consistency—its flavour should be rich with depth and body, and it should have a thick, spooning consistency.

4 Season the sauce with salt and pepper and add a little more sugar if necessary.

to cook in the microwave: combine the olive oil, onion and garlic in a medium microwave-safe bowl. Cook, uncovered, for 4–5 minutes on Medium/500 watts/50%, stirring twice during cooking. Mash or roughly chop the tomatoes. Add the tomatoes with their liquid, tomato paste and sugar to the onion mixture and stir to combine. Cook, uncovered, for 4–5 minutes on High/850watts/100%, followed by 10–15 minutes on Medium/500watts/50%, stirring occasionally. Season to taste with salt and pepper and add a little more sugar if necessary.

This tangy and refreshing chutney is a good one to have on hand. Serve with Indian curries, chargrilled fish, and meats like duck, smoked ham and turkey. It also teams well with vintage cheddar cheese and bread. It will keep unopened in a cool cupboard for up to 6 months. Place it in the fridge once you've opened it where it will keep for up to 3 months.

lime chutney

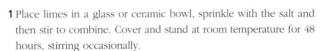

makes: about 1 litre (4 cups)   prep: 15–20 mins (plus 48 hours standing time)   cooking: 1 1/2–2 hours

600g	(about 7) limes, cut into eighths, white core and seeds removed
1 1/2 tbs	salt
1	375g pkt (14 oz) seedless raisins
2 tbs	grated fresh ginger
4	garlic cloves, crushed
300mls	(1 1/3 cups) white wine vinegar
500g	(2 1/2 cups, firmly packed) brown sugar

1 Place limes in a glass or ceramic bowl, sprinkle with the salt and then stir to combine. Cover and stand at room temperature for 48 hours, stirring occasionally.

2 Drain limes and reserve the liquid. Place limes into the bowl of a food processor with the raisins and process until coarsely chopped (it may be necessary to do this in two separate batches).

3 Place the lime and raisin mixture into a large, heavy-based, non-aluminium saucepan. Add the reserved lime liquid, ginger, garlic, vinegar and brown sugar and stir to combine.

4 Bring mixture to the boil. Reduce heat to low and simmer, uncovered, stirring occasionally, for 1 1/2–2 hours or until thick.

5 Spoon chutney into hot sterilised jars (see note) and seal while hot.

note: to sterilise jars, wash jars and lids in warm soapy water and rinse well. Place in a large saucepan and cover with water. Bring to the boil and boil for 10 minutes. Transfer jars and lids to a baking tray lined with baking paper or newspaper and place in an oven preheated to 100°C (220°F) until dry. (If using screw-top lids or ruber gaskets don't put these in the oven—just air-dry them in a colander after boiling them.) Use the jars and lids straight from the oven.

LIMES

- Use lime juice in place of the lemon juice in the recipe for homemade lemonade (p 46).

- Make a lime syrup to spoon over vanilla ice-cream by combining equal quantities of fresh lime juice, water and sugar in a saucepan. Stir over low heat until the sugar dissolves and then bring to the boil. Serve warm or chilled.

- Make a marinade for green prawns by combining 2 tbs fresh lime juice, 1 tbs peanut oil, 1 tsp fish sauce, 1 finely chopped red chilli, 2 crushed garlic cloves, 2 chopped fresh coriander roots, 1 tsp sugar and salt to taste. Marinate for 1 hour and then chargrill or barbecue.

good lime partners: seafood, chilli, fish sauce, coriander, pasta, lemon, ginger, peanut oil.

This dessert makes the most of this heavenly fruit. When buying

figs choose those with a plump body and intense, sweet aroma.

grilled figs
with honey ricotta

serves: 4   prep: 15 mins   cooking: 4–5 mins

8	fresh figs
2 tbs	blanched almonds, finely chopped
2^1/$_2$ tbs	brown sugar
^{1}/$_2$ tsp	ground cinnamon
200g	(7 oz) fresh ricotta
1 tbs	honey
^{1}/$_2$ tsp	vanilla essence

1 Preheat grill on medium-high.

2 Trim the fig stems, cut a cross halfway into the top of each fig and gently ease them open. Place figs into a shallow ovenproof dish.

3 Combine the almonds, brown sugar and cinnamon. Fill each fig cavity evenly with the almond mixture.

4 Place the figs under preheated grill (about 8cm or 3 in from the heat source) and grill for 4–5 minutes or until sugar begins to bubble.

5 Meanwhile, place the ricotta, honey and vanilla essence in a medium bowl and use a wooden spoon to beat until smooth.

6 Place figs and honey ricotta onto serving plates. Serve immediately.

FIGS

■ Cut figs in quarters leaving the bases intact. Drizzle each with 1 tsp honey and then roast in an ovenproof dish for 10 minutes in an oven preheated to 200°C (400°F). Serve with a dollop of thick cream or mascarpone.

■ Combine 250mls (1 cup) orange juice and 110g (^{1}/$_2$ cup) sugar in a small saucepan and stir over medium heat until the sugar dissolves. Bring to the boil and simmer for 5 minutes or until thickened slightly. Stir in 2 tbs orange liqueur and pour over 6 quartered figs in a heat-resistant bowl. Place in the fridge until chilled. Serve with thickened cream. Serves 4.

■ Make a quick fig tart by covering a piece of ready-rolled puff pastry with a layer of sliced figs. Sprinkle with brown sugar and bake in an oven pre-heated to 250°C (475°F) for 10 minutes or until the pastry is crisp and golden. Serve drizzled with thin cream.

good fig partners: ricotta, goat's cheese, honey, prosciutto, raspberries, dark brown sugar, walnuts, almonds.

Good muffin recipes are hard to come by. You can adjust this one depending on the flavourings you prefer. Here are a few variations to get you started.

cinnamon apple muffins

makes: 12   prep: 15 mins   cooking: 20 mins

Melted butter or margarine (optional), for greasing
300g   (2 cups) plain flour
1 tbs   baking powder
2 tsp   ground cinnamon
150g   (3/4 cup, firmly packed) brown sugar
2   medium (about 375g) golden delicious apples, cored, peeled, chopped
145g   (3/4 cup) seedless raisins
125g   (6 tbs) butter, melted, cooled
2   eggs, lightly whisked
185mls   (3/4 cup) milk

1 Preheat oven to 180°C (350°F). You will need 12 medium (125mls/1/2-cup) muffin pans. If you aren't using non-stick pans, brush them lightly with the melted butter or margarine to grease. Alternatively, line the pans with paper muffin cases.
2 Sift together the plain flour, baking powder and cinnamon into a large bowl. Add the brown sugar, apples and raisins and stir to combine.
3 Place the butter, eggs and milk in a medium bowl and use a hand whisk to combine.
4 Add milk mixture to flour mixture and use a large metal spoon to stir until just combined.
5 Spoon the mixture evenly into the muffin pans.
6 Bake in preheated oven for 20 minutes or until golden and cooked through when tested with a skewer. Remove from oven and stand for 2–3 minutes before turning onto a wire rack. Serve warm or at room temperature.

variations

■ **banana & pecan muffins:** replace the apples and raisins with 3 mashed very ripe bananas (combine them with the wet ingredients before adding to the flour mixture) and 100g (2/3 cup) chopped pecan nuts. Reduce the milk to 125mls (1/2 cup). Cook for 25 minutes.

■ **blueberry muffins:** replace apples and raisins with 300g (2 cups) frozen or fresh blueberries and replace the milk with buttermilk. Cook for 20 minutes.

■ **tangy lemon muffins:** replace the cinnamon with finely grated rind of 2 lemons. Replace the brown sugar with 220g (1 cup) caster sugar. Leave out the apples and raisins. Replace the milk with 125mls (1/2 cup) fresh lemon juice and 60g (1/4 cup) natural yoghurt. Cook for 25 minutes.

■ **sweet corn & polenta muffins:** reduce the plain flour to 225g (11/2 cups) and add 170g (1 cup) polenta (cornmeal) with the flour. Leave out the cinnamon and reduce the brown sugar to 50g (1/4 cup, firmly packed). Replace the apples and raisins with a 420g (21/3 cups) can corn kernels, drained. Cook for 20 minutes.

I make this tart all the time. Nobody can ever resist the
sublime, intensley citrus, custard-like filling. I have often made
it with all lemon or all lime juice, depending on what's around.

serves: 8–10   prep: 20 mins (plus 1 hour chilling & 10 mins standing time)   cooking: 50 mins

Icing (powdered) sugar, to serve
Thick (whipped) cream or
vanilla ice-cream, to serve

pastry
225g (1¹/₂ cups) plain flour
180g (9 tbs) butter, chilled, diced
1 tbs caster sugar
2 tbs iced water
1 egg yolk

filling
80mls (¹/₃ cup) fresh lemon juice
80mls (¹/₃ cup) fresh lime juice
165g (³/₄ cup) caster sugar
60mls (¹/₄ cup) thickened cream
5 eggs

1 To make the pastry, place the flour, butter and caster sugar in the bowl of a food processor. Process until the mixture resembles fine breadcrumbs. Lightly whisk together the water and egg yolk and add to the flour mixture. Process briefly until the mixture begins to come together. Remove the pastry from the processor bowl and bring together with your hands. Shape it into a disc and wrap in plastic wrap. Place in the fridge for 30 minutes to rest.

2 Roll out the pastry on a lightly floured bench into a disc about 35cm (14 in) in diameter. Carefully lift the pastry into a 30cm tart tin with removable base and ease it into the tin. Press the pastry gently into the sides. Trim the excess pastry with a sharp knife and then place the lined tin on a baking tray. Place in the fridge for 30 minutes to rest.

3 Preheat oven to 190°C (375°F).

4 Line the tart shell with some greaseproof paper and then fill with rice or dried beans. Bake for 20 minutes in preheated oven. Remove the paper with the rice or beans and bake for a further 10 minutes. Remove from oven and cool for 10 minutes.

5 Meanwhile, to make the filling, place the lemon juice, lime juice, caster sugar and cream in a medium mixing bowl and use a hand whisk to combine. Add the eggs, one at a time, and whisk well after each addition.

6 Pour the filling into the tart shell and bake for a further 20 minutes or until the filling is just set in the centre (it will still wobble slightly when shaken).

7 Serve the tart warm or at room temperature dusted with icing sugar and accompanied by cream or ice-cream.

Looking for a cake to serve with a cup of tea? This is the one for you. It's dense with golden delicious apples and almond meal. Try it served warm with lashings of thick cream for a decadent treat. It will keep at room temperature in an airtight container for up to 3 days.

almond apple cake

serves: 12   prep: 15 mins   cooking: 40 mins

	Melted butter, for greasing
100g	(5 tbs) unsalted butter
110g	($^1/_2$ cup) caster sugar
2	eggs
50g	($^1/_3$ cup) plain flour
1 tsp	baking powder
100g	(1 cup) almond meal
2	golden delicious apples
1 tbs	apricot jam, for glazing

1 Preheat oven to 170°C (340°F). Brush a 20cm springform pan with the melted butter to grease. Line the base of the pan with non-stick baking paper.

2 Use electric beaters to beat the butter and caster sugar in a medium mixing bowl until pale and creamy. Add the eggs one at a time, and beat well after each addition.

3 Sift together the plain flour and baking powder, then stir in the almond meal. Use a large metal spoon to fold the dry ingredients into the butter mixture until combined.

4 Peel, quarter and core apples. Cut each quarter lengthways into thin slices. Use a large metal spoon to carefully fold three quarters of the apple slices into the cake batter. Spoon the mixture into prepared cake pan. Smooth the surface and then arrange the remaining apple slices on top.

5 Bake in preheated oven for 40 minutes or until golden and a skewer inserted in the centre of the cake comes out clean. Stand in pan for 5 minutes before removing the outside of the pan.

6 Place apricot jam in a small saucepan and stir over low heat until melted. Strain and then brush over the top of the warm cake. Serve warm or at room temperature.

This mousse is smooth, rich and very addictive. If the coffee isn't hot enough to melt the chocolate, pop it in a heat-resistant bowl over simmering water or in a microwave-safe, glass or ceramic bowl. Heat uncovered for 1 minute on High/850watts/100%, and then stir until smooth.

decadent chocolate mousse

serves: 8   prep: 10–15 mins (plus 2 hours chilling time)

PASSIONFRUIT

- Top pavlova with whipped cream, banana and lots of passionfruit pulp.
- Sweeten passionfruit pulp with a little sugar, warm and spoon over vanilla ice-cream.
- Make a passionfruit icing for a sponge or butter cake by combining 300g (2 cups) sifted pure icing (powdered) sugar, pulp from 2 passionfruit and 10g (2 tsp) butter in a heat resistant bowl. Stir over simmering water until shiny and smooth. Use immediately.

good passionfruit partners: bananas, vanilla ice-cream, natural yoghurt, oranges, mangoes.

250g	(9 oz) good quality dark chocolate, finely chopped
80mls	($^1/_3$ cup) freshly made strong black coffee
3	eggs, separated
2 tbs	caster sugar
185mls	($^3/_4$ cup) thickened cream

1 Place chocolate in a large bowl and pour the coffee over. Stand for 1 minute and then stir until the chocolate melts.

2 Add the egg yolks to the chocolate mixture and use a wooden spoon to beat until combined.

3 Whisk the egg whites with electric beaters or hand whisk until soft peaks form. Sprinkle the caster sugar over the egg whites and whisk until thick and glossy. Use a metal spoon to fold a large spoonful of the egg white mixture into the chocolate mixture until combined. Fold in the remaining egg whites.

4 Use electric beaters or a hand whisk to beat the cream in a medium bowl until soft peaks form. Fold into the chocolate mixture until well combined.

5 Spoon the mousse into a 1-litre (4-cup) serving dish or eight 125mls ($^1/_2$-cup) individual dishes or glasses. Cover with plastic wrap and place in the fridge for at least 2 hours before serving.

These crisp, buttery, oaty biscuits are reminiscent of the traditional Scottish oatmeal biscuits. They are slightly sweet and are a perfect partner for a creamy blue vein cheese (like Blue Castello). Serve at afternoon tea, with drinks or after dinner. The oat biscuits will keep in an airtight container for up to a week.

oat biscuits
served with blue vein cheese & pears

serves: 6 (makes about 18 biscuits)　prep: 15 mins (plus 15 mins chilling time)　cooking: 25 mins

3	pears (like beurre bosc or packham), to serve
1 tbs	fresh lemon juice
150g	($1/_2$ cup) creamy blue vein cheese, to serve

oat biscuits

170g	(2 cups) 1-Minute Oats
75g	($1/_2$ cup) plain flour
$1^1/_2$ tbs	brown sugar
$1/_4$ tsp	baking powder
$1/_4$ tsp	salt
100g	(5 tbs) unsalted butter, melted, cooled
60mls	($1/_4$ cup) water

1 To make the oat biscuits, preheat oven to 180°C (350°F). Line 2 baking trays with non-stick baking paper.

2 Combine the oats, plain flour, brown sugar, baking powder and salt in a medium bowl and mix well. Add the butter and water and use a round-bladed knife to stir until combined. Bring the mixture together with your fingertips to form a dough.

3 Divide dough into 2 equal portions. Roll one portion out on a lightly floured surface to about 5mm thick. Use a 6cm-round fluted cutter to cut out biscuits and then place them on the lined baking trays. Repeat with the remaining portion of dough. Place the biscuits in the fridge to chill for 15 minutes.

4 Bake the biscuits in preheated oven for 25 minutes or until golden. Remove from the oven and cool on the trays. Store in an airtight container until required.

5 Just before serving, core pears and cut into thin wedges. Toss with lemon juice to prevent discolouration. Serve the oat biscuits with pear wedges and the blue vein cheese.

These crunchy cookies will hit the spot with peanut butter lovers. They keep in an air-tight jar for up to 1 week. For a soft fudge centre, cook each batch for 10–12 minutes.

peanut butter cookies

makes: about 40   prep: 15 mins   cooking: 15 mins (for each batch)

125g (9 tbs) butter, at room temperature
275g (1 cup) crunchy peanut butter
200g (1 cup, firmly packed) brown sugar
1 egg
260g (1³/₄ cups) plain flour
¹/₂ tsp baking powder
120g (³/₄ cup) unsalted roasted
       peanuts, roughly chopped

1 Preheat oven to 180°C (350°F). Line a baking tray with non-stick baking paper.

2 Use electric beaters to beat butter and peanut butter in a large mixing bowl until creamy. Add the brown sugar and beat until pale. Add egg and beat until combined.

3 Sift together the plain flour and baking powder. Use a wooden spoon to mix the dry ingredients and peanuts into the peanut butter mixture.

4 Lightly flour your hands then roll tablespoonfuls of the biscuit mixture into balls and place about 4cm (1.5 in) apart on the lined baking tray. Flatten each ball to about 5cm (2 in) in diameter and 1cm thick.

5 Bake in preheated oven for 15 minutes or until golden and cooked through. Stand on baking tray for 5 minutes before transferring to a wire rack to cool. Repeat with the remaining mixture.

APPLES

■ **baking:** golden delicious, pink lady, royal gala and jonagold.

■ **poaching:** golden delicious, royal gala, pink lady and granny smith.

■ **tarts, pies and cakes:** golden delicious, lady williams, jonagold, sundowner and jonathan.

■ **apple sauce and puree:** bonza and granny smith.

■ **only eating:** red delicious and breaburn (plus all of the above).

good apple partners: brown sugar, golden syrup, walnuts, pecans, pork, raisins, mixed spice, cinnamon, pastry.

fresh date & bran loaf with vanilla yoghurt spread

serves: 10–12   prep: 15 mins   cooking: 50 mins

	Melted butter, for greasing
150g	(1 cup) plain flour
1 tsp	baking powder
1 tsp	bicarbonate of soda (baking soda)
1 tsp	ground cinnamon
	Pinch of salt
100g	(1/2 cup, firmly packed) brown sugar
210g	(2 cups) unprocessed bran
100g	(1/2 cup) coarsely chopped pitted fresh dates
90g	(1/2 cup) chopped dried figs
60g	(3 tbs) butter, melted
1 tbs	golden syrup
1	egg, lightly whisked
250mls	(1 cup) milk

1 Preheat oven to 180°C (350°F). Brush an 9 x 19cm or 3.5 x 8 in (base measurement) loaf pan with the melted butter to grease and line the base with non-stick baking paper.

2 Sift together the plain flour, baking powder, bicarbonate of soda, cinnamon and salt into a large bowl. Add the brown sugar, unprocessed bran, dates and figs and use your hands to toss lightly to combine.

3 Whisk together the melted butter, golden syrup, egg and milk until well combined. Add to the bran mixture and use a wooden spoon to stir until combined.

4 Spoon the mixture into the prepared loaf pan and bake in preheated oven for 50 minutes or until a skewer inserted into the centre of the loaf comes out clean. Remove from the oven and turn onto a wire rack to cool. Serve at room temperature with the vanilla yoghurt spread. Keep in an airtight container at room temperature for up to 3 days.

vanilla yoghurt spread

makes: about 2 cups   prep: 5 mins
(plus 24 hours standing time)

500g	(2 cups) thick natural yoghurt
2 tbs	honey
2 tsp	vanilla essence

1 Line a sieve with a double layer of muslin or a loosely woven tea towel and then place it over a large bowl (to allow for drainage).

2 Place the yoghurt, honey and vanilla essence in a bowl and use a wooden spoon to combine. Spoon yoghurt mixture into the lined sieve.

3 Place in the fridge for 24 hours or until enough liquid whey has drained away to make the yoghurt a thick, spreadable consistency. Discard the liquid whey and transfer the yoghurt spread to an airtight container. Keep for up to 1 week in the fridge.

Homely bread & butter pudding wasn't a dessert I grew

up with, but I'm making up for lost time. This recipe

utilises hot cross buns in a unique but brilliant way over

Easter. The inclusion of marmalade adds a lovely zing.

Easter bread & butter pudding

serves: 6   prep: 10–15 mins (plus 25–40 mins standing time)   cooking: 35–40 mins

4	hot cross buns
60g	(3 tbs) butter
170g	(1/2 cup) orange marmalade
2	eggs
75g	(1/3 cup) sugar
500mls	(2 cups) milk
250mls	(1 cup) thin cream
1/4 tsp	ground nutmeg
	Vanilla ice-cream or
	thick (whipped) cream, to serve

1 Cut each hot cross bun into three slices to make 12 slices in total. Spread one side of each slice with butter and then marmalade.

2 Layer the slices in a 14 x 26cm or 5.5 x 10 in (base measurement) (1.5-litre/6-cup) ovenproof dish.

3 Combine the eggs, sugar, milk, cream and nutmeg in a jug and use a hand whisk to combine. Pour the mixture evenly over the sliced hot cross buns. Stand for 20–30 minutes or until the milk mixture is absorbed.

4 Meanwhile, preheat oven to 180°C (350°F).

5 Bake the pudding in preheated oven for 35–40 minutes or until golden and just firm.

6 Remove from the oven and stand for 5–10 minutes. Serve with the ice-cream or cream.

winter

a season for foods with heart and soul

There are many vegetables that adore the cold. Some of my favourites are fennel, Jerusalem artichokes, silverbeet and English spinach. Sauté them, roast them, braise them. In winter they're at their peak.

Australia is one of the few countries in the world where potatoes are available all year round. But, personally, I think spuds are most suited to cool-weather cooking. Potatoes are grown everywhere: the Atherton Tablelands in Queensland, Hillstone in New South Wales, Thorpdale in Victoria, the coastal areas of Tasmania, Mount Gambier in South Australia and Gin Gin in Western Australia (just to mention a few). The supply for the markets follows a pattern set by the cool, frost-free weather.

Spuds can be mashed with garlic-infused milk and enriched with lashings of butter, and maybe some cream, and piled high on your plate. They can be baked whole in their jackets until the flesh is fluffy, then topped with a dollop of sour cream. You can rub potatoes generously with olive oil and salt and roast them in wedges to a crisp, golden state. You can layer them with egg, cream and milk and bake or boil them whole and then coat them with lots of salty butter and herbs.

Recently, a whole new wave of potato varieties have appeared in Australia: king edward, pink fir apple, kipfler and nicola to name a few. Each has its own characteristics and it is important to choose a potato to suit the task. Generally speaking, 'floury' potatoes (high in starch and low in moisture) are ideal for baking, roasting, mashing and chipping. 'Waxy' varieties are higher in moisture and great for boiling,

adding to casseroles and making salads as they won't fall apart easily when cooked this way. Then there are the all-purpose potatoes, specifically bred to be all-rounders. Use our chart as a quick guide.

Citrus also shines in winter—lemons, navel oranges, tangelos, pomelos, cumquats and mandarins. My husband and I joke that we bought our house purely for the lemon tree out the back (the mandarin tree down the side was a bonus). These trees not only keep our fruit bowl full but the leaves impart a heavenly scent when rubbed between the fingers and the branches fill vases with attractive glossy leaves when flowers are scarce.

which potato?

	nicola	bintje	spunta	desiree	russet burbank (idaho)	king edward	jersey royal	pink fir apple	pink eye	kipfler	rosevale	coliban (washed)	sebago (brushed)	pontiac
mash	■■	■	■■■	■■	■	■■■			■■■	■■			■■	■■■
boil	■■■	■■	■■	■■■			■■■	■■■	■■■	■■■	■■■	■■■	■■	■■
roast	■■	■■■	■■		■■■	■■■		■■		■■		■■	■■■	■■
bake	■■	■■■	■■	■■	■■■	■■■		■■		■■		■	■■	■■
chip/wedge	■■	■■■	■■	■■	■■■	■■■		■		■			■■	■■
salad	■■■	■■	■		■		■■■	■■■	■■	■■■	■■■	■■		

■ good   ■■ very good   ■■■ the best

winter's best
a guide to help you use produce at the height of its season

vegetables

- artichokes:
  globe (late)
  Jerusalem
- Asian greens:
  choy sum
- asparagus (late)
- beans:
  borlotti
  broad (fava or lima) (late)
  green
- beetroot (beet)
- broccoli
- brussels sprouts
- cabbage
- carrots
- cauliflower
- celeriac (celery root)
- celery
- chillies
- fennel
- garlic
- ginger
- kohlrabi (early)
- leeks
- lettuce
- mushrooms
  (cultivated)

- onions:
  brown
  green shallots/green
  onions/scallions/French
  shallots/eschallots
  red/Spanish
  spring
  white
- parsnip
- peas:
  green (mid to late)
  snow (late)
  sugar snap (early to late)
- potatoes (general)
- pumpkin
- radish (mid to late)
- rhubarb
- silverbeet
- spinach/English
  spinach
- squash (early)
- swede
- sweet potato
- turnip
- witlof (chicory) (early)
- zucchini

This information may vary slightly depending on
where you live and/or weather conditions

fruit

- apples:
  bonza
  braeburn (early to mid)
  fuji
  golden delicious
  granny smith
  jonathan (early to mid)
  lady williams (mid to late)
  pink lady
  red delicious
  sundowner
- avocados
- bananas
- berries:
  strawberries
  (mid to late)
- carambola
  (star fruit)
- cumquat (late)
- custard apple

- grapefruit:
  pink (mid to late)
- lemons
- mandarins
- nashi
- oranges:
  navel
  seville (mid to late)
  blood (late)
- passionfruit
  (early to mid)
- pears:
  beurre bosc
  packham
- pomelos
- quince (early)
- tamarillo (mid)
- tangelos (mid to late)

garlic & potato pizza

serves: 4 as an appetiser   prep: 10 mins   cooking: 15 mins

4	garlic cloves
	Salt & ground black pepper, to taste
80mls	($1/3$ cup) olive oil
1	25cm (10 in) Lebanese bread round
2	medium (about 320g) desiree potatoes, thinly sliced
$1/2$	bunch fresh thyme, leaves picked

1 Preheat oven to 220°C (424°F). Line a baking tray with non-stick baking paper.

2 Finely chop 2 of the garlic cloves. Sprinkle the chopped garlic with a pinch of salt and then crush with the flat side of a knife blade. Combine the garlic and 2 tbs of the olive oil in a small bowl. Place the Lebanese bread on the lined baking tray and brush with the garlic oil.

3 Finely slice the remaining garlic cloves, and combine with the sliced potatoes in a medium bowl. Add the remaining olive oil and thyme leaves. Season with salt and pepper and toss thoroughly to combine.

4 Arrange the potato and garlic mixture over the bread. Drizzle with any remaining olive oil and thyme leaves.

5 Bake in preheated oven for 15 minutes or until golden and the potatoes are tender. Serve warm.

orange & fennel salad

serves: 4 as an accompaniment   prep: 15 mins

4 oranges
2 small (about 600g) fennel bulbs, trimmed, finely sliced
1 medium red onion, finely sliced
1/4 cup loosely packed, continental parsley leaves

orange & mustard dressing
100mls olive oil
80mls (1/3 cup) fresh orange juice
1 tsp wholegrain mustard
Salt & ground black pepper, to taste

1 Finely grate the rind from 1 orange and reserve. Peel and segment all the oranges.

2 To make the dressing, combine the reserved orange rind, olive oil, orange juice, mustard and salt and pepper in a screw-top jar. Shake well.

3 Place the orange segments, fennel and onion in a bowl and toss to combine.

4 Place the salad on a serving plate or in a bowl, sprinkle with the parsley and pour the orange dressing over.

This salad makes the most of winter's avocados. The best way to tell if an avocado is ripe is to press it gently at the stem end—if it yields slightly it is ready to eat. Avoid fruit that has any sunken or dark spots and remember that ripe avocados bruise very easily.

avocado & prawn salad

serves: 4 as an entree   prep: 15 mins

2   ripe avocados
12   (about 400g) medium cooked prawns,
       peeled with tails left intact, deveined
1/4 bunch fresh chives, cut into 2.5cm lengths
       Salt & ground black pepper, to taste

creamy orange dressing
3 tbs   good quality mayonnaise
1   orange, rind finely grated
60mls   (1/4 cup) fresh orange juice

1 To make the dressing, place the mayonnaise and orange rind and juice in a small bowl and stir to combine.
2 Halve, deseed and peel the avocados. Cut each avocado half lengthways into thirds.
3 Place three avocado slices on each serving plate, top with 3 prawns and spoon the dressing over. Sprinkle with the chives, salt and pepper. Serve immediately.

prawn & noodle soup with coriander paste

serves: 4 prep: 25-30 mins cooking: 8-10 mins

1	250g pkt (9 oz) dried Chinese (wheat) noodles
2 tsp	vegetable oil
1.25 L	(5 cups) good-quality chicken stock
16	(about 300g) medium green prawns, peeled with tails left intact, deveined
60mls	(1/4 cup) fish sauce
2 tbs	fresh lime juice
1	large carrot, halved lengthways, thinly sliced
2	green shallots, thinly sliced
1/4 cup	fresh coriander leaves

coriander paste

1/3 cup	chopped fresh coriander roots and stems
1	garlic clove, crushed
1 tsp	grated fresh ginger
1	small fresh red chilli, chopped
1 tbs	fresh lime juice

1 To make the coriander paste, combine the coriander roots and stems, garlic, ginger, chilli and lime juice in the bowl of a food processor and process until a paste forms. Scrape the sides of the bowl when necessary. (Alternatively, use a mortar and pestle.) Transfer the paste to a bowl and cover the surface closely with plastic wrap to prevent it from discolouring.

2 Cook the noodles in a large saucepan of boiling water for 5 minutes or following packet directions, until tender. Drain and rinse under hot water. Place in a large bowl and toss with the vegetable oil. Cover with foil, set aside and keep warm.

3 Bring the stock to the boil in a large saucepan. Reduce heat to medium, add the prawns and simmer for 1 minute or until they change colour and are just cooked through. Remove the prawns from the stock with a slotted spoon. Remove the saucepan from the heat and add the fish sauce and lime juice to the stock.

4 Separate the noodles and divide them among 4 serving bowls. Top with the carrot, green shallots and prawns. Ladle the hot stock over, sprinkle with coriander leaves and top with a spoonful of the coriander paste.

GARLIC

■ Make an aioli by processing 4 egg yolks and 1 tsp Dijon mustard until combined. With the motor running, gradually add 250mls (1 cup) olive oil drop by drop until the mixture begins to thicken. Add any remaining oil in a very thin, steady stream until well combined. Stir in 2 tbs fresh lemon juice and 4 crushed garlic cloves. Season well with salt and pepper. A perfect partner for seafood—especially prawns and poached salmon.

■ Combine 50g (2 1/2 tbs) softened butter with 3 crushed garlic cloves and 1 tbs chopped fresh chives. Spread on a French stick split lengthways, wrap in foil and heat in an oven preheated to 180°C (350°F) for 10-15 minutes or until the butter has melted and the bread is heated through.

■ Quickly cook some finely chopped garlic, red chilli and anchovies in plenty of olive oil in a large saucepan over medium heat until the anchovies start to dissolve. Add drained cooked thin spaghetti and lots of chopped fresh parsley and black pepper. Toss to combine and serve with crusty bread.

good garlic partners: lemon, roast lamb, anchovies, rosemary, chickpeas (see recipes for hummus p 68 and chickpea & garlic puree p 40), chilli, olive oil, butter, fresh herbs, veal, chicken.

crispy fish & chips
with tartare sauce

serves: 4   prep: 20-25 mins   cooking: 40-45 mins

Canola or vegetable oil, for deep frying

4 (about 225g or 1/2 pound each) firm, white fish fillets (like ling)
Self-raising flour, for coating

tartare sauce

250mls (1 cup) basic mayonnaise (recipe below) or good-quality purchased mayonnaise
1/2 lemon, rind finely grated, juiced
1 gherkin, chopped
2 tsp chopped drained capers
1 tbs chopped fresh parsley

chips

6 large (about 300g or 10 oz each) potatoes (like russet burbank/idaho or sebago/brushed)

beer batter

150g (1 cup) self-raising flour
Pinch of salt
1 egg, lightly whisked
250mls (1 cup) beer

1 To make the tartare sauce, place the prepared mayonnaise, lemon rind, 1 tbs lemon juice, gherkin, capers and parsley in a small bowl and stir to combine. Cover and set aside.

2 To make the chips, peel the potatoes and cut into batons about 8cm (3 in) long and 1cm thick. Use a clean tea towel or paper towel to remove any excess moisture from the surface of the potatoes.

3 Meanwhile, heat the canola or vegetable oil in a large saucepan over medium heat or in a deep-fryer to 190°C (375°F) or until a chip dropped into the hot oil sizzles immediately and rises to the surface. Add about one third of the chips and cook for 5–8 minutes or until lightly golden. Drain on paper towel and repeat with remaining chips. Set aside.

4 To make the beer batter, combine the self-raising flour and salt in a bowl. Make a well in the centre, add the egg and beer and stir, gradually incorporating the flour, to form a smooth batter.

5 Reheat the oil to 190°C (375°F) and return all the chips to the saucepan or deep-fryer for about 5 minutes or until golden and crisp.

6 Meanwhile, lightly dust the fish pieces in the flour to coat. Set aside.

7 Drain the chips on paper towel and set aside to keep warm.

8 Reheat the oil to 190°C (375°F) or until a little of the batter dropped into the hot oil sizzles and rises to the surface. Cut the fillets into 3 equal pieces. Coat the fish pieces with the batter and then carefully transfer to the hot oil, 3 pieces at a time, and cook for about 3 minutes or until the fish is just cooked and the batter is golden and crisp. Drain on paper towel and keep warm. Repeat with the remaining fish.

9 Serve fish and chips immediately accompanied by the tartare sauce and some lemon wedges, if desired.

basic mayonnaise
makes: about 500mls (2 cups)   prep: 15-20 mins

4 large egg yolks
2 tbs fresh lemon juice or white wine vinegar
2 tsp Dijon mustard
Salt & ground black pepper, to taste
400mls (1 1/2 cup) olive oil

1 Place the egg yolks, lemon juice or vinegar, Dijon mustard, salt and pepper into the bowl of a food processor. Process until creamy and the mixture starts to thicken.

2 With the motor running add the oil gradually, no more than 1 tsp at a time. Blend well after each addition until the oil is thoroughly incorporated before adding the next lot.

3 Once the mayonnaise starts to thicken and hold its shape, slowly pour the remaining oil from a jug in a thin steady stream into the mayonnaise with the motor running until all the oil is incorporated.

4 Check seasoning and add more lemon juice or vinegar and salt and pepper if needed.

warm pumpkin
spinach & feta salad

serves: 4-6 as an accompaniment   prep: 10 mins   cooking: 10–15 mins

1/2   medium (about 650g) butternut pumpkin,
      peeled, deseeded, cut into 1cm cubes
2 tbs   olive oil
45g   (1/4 cup) pine nuts
1   small red onion, thinly sliced
1 tsp   paprika
1   bunch English spinach, trimmed, washed
1   orange, juiced
120g   (1/2 cup) Greek feta, cubed

1 Cook the pumpkin in a saucepan of salted boiling water over high heat for 3–5 minutes or until just tender but still firm to the bite. Drain and refresh under cold running water.

2 Heat the olive oil in a large frying pan over medium heat and cook the pine nuts, stirring occasionally, for 1–2 minutes or until golden. Remove the pine nuts from the pan and drain on paper towel.

3 Add the onion to the pan and cook over medium heat for 5 minutes or until just soft. Stir in pumpkin and paprika and cook, stirring gently, for 1 minute or until aromatic. Stir in the spinach and orange juice and cook, stirring occasionally, for 2–3 minutes or until the spinach is just wilted.

4 Gently stir in the pine nuts and feta. Serve warm.

JERUSALEM ARTICHOKES

■ Use a small sharp knife to peel Jerusalem artichokes—you will find it a lot easier than using a vegetable peeler. But leave the skin on if you wish—it will add colour and flavour.

■ To make a simple soup, cook 2 sliced medum leeks and 2 crushed garlic cloves in about 40g (2 tbs) butter in a saucepan over medium heat for 3–5 minutes. Cut 750g (1 1/2 pounds) scrubbed Jerusalem artichokes into 1cm pieces and add them to the leeks with 1 tsp ground nutmeg and cook for a further 5 minutes. Then stir in 750mls (3 cups) chicken or vegetable stock and boil gently for 15 minutes or until the artichokes are tender. Puree in 2 separate batches. Stir in 3 tbs sour cream and gently heat through. Serve sprinkled with chopped fresh chives.

■ Sauté, sliced, unpeeled Jerusalem artichokes in a little butter over medium heat until tender. Add a little chopped garlic and cook for a further 1 minute. Drizzle with some lemon juice, toss through some chopped fresh parsley and serve immediately. A wonderful accompaniment for chicken or veal.

■ Peel some Jerusalem artichokes, cut them into 2–3cm lengths and then toss them with a little olive oil and sea salt. Spread them in a roasting pan and roast in an oven preheated to 250°C (475°F) for about 15 minutes or until tender.

good Jerusalem artichoke partners: olive oil, butter, cream, garlic, silverbeet, lemon, veal, English spinach, chicken, nutmeg, chives, leeks, parsley, walnuts, hazelnuts, root vegetables.

country-style soup with italian sausage

serves: 4–6   prep: 10–15 mins   cooking: 35–40 mins

2 tbs	olive oil
2	fresh Italian-style sausages
2	leeks, trimmed, chopped, washed
2	garlic cloves, crushed
2 tsp	dried oregano
2 tsp	dried basil
6	chat (small washed) potatoes, halved
2	carrots, peeled, cut into batons 1.5cm-thick and 4cm long
2	celery sticks, chopped
1	400g can whole peeled tomatoes, drained, chopped
750mls	(3 cups) beef stock
250mls	(1 cup) water
2	zucchini, diagonally sliced
	Salt & ground black pepper, to taste
	Shaved parmesan, to serve
	Fresh continental parsley sprigs (optional), to garnish

1 Heat half the olive oil in a large saucepan over medium heat and cook the whole sausages for about 8–10 minutes or until browned and cooked through. Remove sausages from the saucepan and drain on paper towel.

2 Heat the remaining olive oil in the saucepan over medium heat and cook the leeks, garlic, oregano and basil, stirring occasionally, for 5 minutes or until the leeks are soft.

3 Add the potatoes and cook for 8 minutes, stirring occasionally. Add the carrots, celery, tomatoes, beef stock and water. Bring to the boil over medium heat.

4 Cut the sausages diagonally into 2cm- or ca. 1 in-thick slices and add to the soup with zucchini. Reduce the heat and simmer for 5–10 minutes or until the vegetables are tender.

5 Season with salt and pepper. Serve topped with the shaved parmesan and garnished with the parsley sprigs, if desired.

Lentils are believed to have originated in Syria and are a popular staple in the Middle East and India. Brown lentils (sometimes called green lentils), unlike yellow or red lentils, hold their shape after cooking, making them a good base for dishes such as this vegetarian ragout.

Middle Eastern lentil & root vegetable spiced ragout

serves: 6   prep: 15 mins   cooking: 35–40 mins

165g	($^3/_4$ cup) brown lentils
2 tbs	olive oil
2	brown onions, finely chopped
2	garlic cloves, crushed
2 tsp	grated fresh ginger
$^1/_2$ tsp	ground cinnamon
1 tsp	ground turmeric
1 tsp	cayenne pepper
$^1/_4$	(about 400g or $^3/_4$ pound) cauliflower, cut into small florets
300g	(14 oz) deseeded pumpkin, peeled, cubed
2	carrots, peeled, cubed
2	turnips, peeled, cubed
2	parsnips, peeled, cubed
$^1/_2$	red capsicum (pepper), quartered, deseeded, cubed
250mls	(1 cup) vegetable stock
1	400g (14 oz) can peeled whole tomatoes, drained, chopped
2	whole cloves
	Salt & ground black pepper, to taste
	Couscous, prepared following packet directions, to serve

1 Place the lentils in a sieve and rinse well under cold running water. Transfer them to a medium saucepan and cover generously with water. Bring to the boil, reduce heat to medium-low and simmer for 25–30 minutes or until tender. Add more water during cooking if needed. Drain and set aside.

2 Meanwhile, heat olive oil in a large heavy-based saucepan over medium heat and cook the onions, garlic, ginger, cinnamon, turmeric and cayenne pepper for 5–8 minutes or until the onions are soft and the mixture is aromatic.

3 Add the cauliflower, pumpkin, carrots, turnips, parsnips and capsicum, and cook for 5 minutes. Stir in stock, tomatoes and cloves and bring to the boil. Reduce heat and simmer gently, uncovered, for 20 minutes or until vegetables are tender.

4 Add the lentils to the vegetables and simmer for 2 minutes or until heated through. Season with salt and pepper and serve over the couscous.

You can make this economical dish up to the end of step 4 one day ahead. Cool it and

keep it in an airtight container in the fridge. To reheat it, place the chicken in a large

saucepan and cook over a low heat for about 30 minutes or until heated through.

braised chicken
with tomato capers & olives

s e r v e s : 8 p r e p : 2 0 m i n s c o o k i n g : 6 0 – 6 5 m i n s

2 tbs	olive oil
1	150g (5 oz) jar capers, drained well on paper towel
16	(about 3.3kg or 7 pounds) chicken thigh pieces with the skin on, backbone and excess fat removed
2	garlic cloves, crushed
750mls	(3 cups) chicken stock
3	400g (14 oz) cans peeled whole tomatoes, undrained
200g	(1 cup) kalamata olives, halved, pitted
1	bunch continental parsley, leaves roughly chopped
	Salt & ground black pepper, to taste
	Cumin roasted potatoes (recipe right), to serve
	Warm crusty bread, to serve

1 Heat $1^{1}/_{2}$ tbs olive oil in a large, wide saucepan over medium-high heat. Add the capers and cook for 3–4 minutes or until slightly crisp. Remove from the pan with a slotted spoon and set aside.

2 Add the remaining olive oil and heat over medium-high heat. Add 6 of the chicken pieces, skin side down and cook for 2 minutes on each side or until golden. Remove the chicken from the pan. Repeat in 2 more batches with the remaining chicken. Discard any excess oil left in the pan.

3 Return all the chicken to the pan with the garlic. Increase heat to high, pour half the stock over the chicken and bring to the boil. Boil, uncovered, for 3 minutes.

4 Add the remaining stock, undrained tomatoes, olives and capers and return to the boil. Reduce heat to medium and simmer, uncovered, for 30 minutes or until the chicken is tender.

5 Remove the chicken from the pan and set aside. Increase heat to high and simmer, uncovered, for 10 minutes or until the sauce is reduced and thickened slightly. Reduce heat to medium-low and return the chicken to the pan. Cook for 4–5 minutes or until the chicken is heated through.

6 Stir in the parsley and season with salt and pepper. Serve with the cumin roasted potatoes and warm crusty bread.

cumin roasted potatoes

s e r v e s : 8 p r e p : 1 5 m i n s
c o o k i n g : 4 5 m i n s

125mls	($^{1}/_{2}$ cup) olive oil
$1^{1}/_{2}$ tbs	ground cumin
1 tsp	salt
2.5kg	(5.5 pounds) sebago (brushed) potatoes, peeled, cut into 2.5cm (1 in) cubes
	Salt & ground black pepper, to taste

1 Preheat oven to 200°C (400°F).

2 Combine olive oil, ground cumin and salt in a small bowl. Divide oil mixture evenly between two roasting pans large enough to hold the potatoes in a single layer. Place the pans in preheated oven and heat oil for 4 minutes, watching carefully so the oil doesn't burn.

3 Carefully remove the roasting pans from the oven. Divide the potatoes evenly between the pans and toss gently to coat in the oil.

4 Return the pans to the oven and roast the potatoes for 20 minutes. Swap pans around in the oven, and roast for a further 20 minutes or until golden and crisp. Toss the potatoes twice during cooking to help them brown evenly. Season well with salt and pepper and serve immediately.

Malaysian chicken curry

serves: 4–6   prep: 10 mins   cooking: 1¼ hours

1	brown onion, quartered
2	garlic cloves, peeled
3cm	(about 1 in) piece fresh ginger, peeled
1	drained canned tomato, quartered
1	birdseye chilli
1 tsp	purchased Madras curry paste
60mls	(¹/₄ cup) vegetable oil
2 tsp	ground turmeric
2 tsp	salt
1kg	chicken drumsticks
1	400ml (16 oz) can coconut cream
	Cooked jasmine rice, to serve
	Steamed Asian greens (like bok choy), to serve

1 Preheat oven to 180°C (350°F).

2 Place the onion, garlic, ginger, tomato, chilli, curry paste and 1 tbs of the vegetable oil in the bowl of a food processor and process until the mixture forms a paste.

3 Combine the turmeric and salt in a bowl and sprinkle evenly over the drumsticks to coat.

4 Heat remaining vegetable oil in a large heavy-based frying pan over medium-high heat and cook the drumsticks, turning occasionally, for 5–8 minutes or until golden. Place drumsticks in a single layer in an ovenproof dish. Set aside.

5 Add the onion paste to the frying pan and cook over medium heat for 5 minutes or until aromatic. Stir in the coconut cream and bring just to the boil.

6 Pour the mixture over the drumsticks and then cover the dish with a lid or a piece of foil. Cook in preheated oven for 1 hour. Turn the drumsticks after 30 minutes.

7 Serve the curry accompanied by the jasmine rice and steamed Asian greens.

roast loin of pork

erves: 6   prep: 20 mins   cooking: 1 1/2 hours

1   1.5kg (3 pounds) rolled boned pork loin
1 tbs   salt
6   evenly sized medium potatoes (like sebago/brushed, bintje or desiree), washed
6   parsnips, halved lengthways
6   medium zucchini, ends trimmed

wine sauce
125mls   (1/2 cup) red or white wine
250mls   (1 cup) beef or chicken stock
1–2 tbs   redcurrant jelly, to taste
Salt & ground black pepper, to taste

1 Remove the pork loin from the fridge and bring to room temperature. Preheat oven to 250°C (475°F).

2 Cut evenly spaced, parallel slits 1–2 cm (1/2 in) apart in the skin of the pork. Rub the salt well into the surface (this will make the skin crackle). Place the pork in a flameproof roasting pan large enough to hold the pork and the vegetables around it. Roast the pork in preheated oven for 20–25 minutes.

3 Halve potatoes. Remove roasting pan from oven, add potatoes to the pan around the pork and turn them to coat with a little fat from the bottom of the pan. Reduce the oven temperature to 200°C (400F) and roast for 30 minutes.

4 Remove pan from the oven again and add the parsnips and coat them in fat as you did with the potatoes. Roast for 15 minutes. Turn vegetables again, add the whole zucchini and coat with fat. Roast for a further 15 minutes or until the pork is just cooked and the vegetables are tender.

5 Place the pork on a carving plate or board and set aside, uncovered, in a warm place to rest. Transfer the vegetables to an ovenproof dish and return to the oven while making the sauce.

6 To make the sauce, use a large metal spoon to skim any fat from the surface of the juices in the roasting pan. Place the pan over medium-high heat, add the wine and bring to the boil. Use a wooden spoon to scrape the pan to dislodge any tasty residue on the base so that it becomes part of the sauce. Add stock and boil until reduced by half. Add redcurrant jelly and stir until dissolved. Season with salt and pepper.

7 Carve the pork loin by using the cuts in the crackling as a guide. Discard the string that holds the roast together as you carve. Serve with the vegetables and the sauce.

Ask your butcher to bone, roll and tie a pork loin. Pork is best when it is just cooked through, not overdone. An easy test is to insert a skewer into the centre of the loin—if the juices run clear it is ready to take from the oven.

roast lamb
with pink grapefruit

serves: 6-8   prep: 10-15 mins   cooking: 1 1/2-1 3/4 hours

1	1.5kg (3 pounds) leg of lamb
4	garlic cloves, quartered
185mls	(3/4 cup) honey
250mls	(1 cup) fresh grapefruit juice (from pink or yellow grapefruit)
	Salt & ground black pepper, to taste
3	bunches spring onions, roots and stems trimmed
3	pink grapefruit, segmented
375mls	(1 1/2 cups) chicken or vegetable stock

1 Preheat oven to 180°C (350°F).

2 Use a small sharp knife to make 16 shallow slits in the surface of the lamb. Insert a garlic quarter into each slit. Place the lamb in a flameproof roasting pan.

3 Combine the honey and grapefruit juice in a bowl and stir until smooth. Brush the lamb generously with the grapefruit juice mixture and sprinkle with salt and pepper.

4 Roast lamb in preheated oven for 45 minutes, basting with pan juices and grapefruit juice mixture every 15 minutes. Place the spring onions in the roasting pan around the lamb and roast for a further 35 minutes, basting every 15 minutes. Add the pink grapefruit segments to the roasting pan and roast for a further 10 minutes.

5 Remove pan from oven and transfer the lamb, spring onions and grapefruit segments to a warm platter. Cover loosely with foil and stand in a warm place for at least 10 minutes for the lamb to rest.

6 Meanwhile, use a large metal spoon to skim as much fat as possible from the surface of the juices remaining in the roasting pan. Stir in the stock and season with salt and pepper. Place the roasting pan on the stove top and bring to the boil. Reduce heat and simmer, uncovered, stirring often, for 5 minutes or until reduced by one third.

7 Serve the lamb with the spring onions, grapefruit segments and the grapefruit sauce.

winter salad

serves: 8 prep: 10 mins cooking: 7 mins

6	(about 75g) thin slices prosciutto
280g	(1²/₃ cups) snow peas, topped
2	ripe avocados
3	large radicchio lettuces, outer leaves discarded, leaves separated, washed, dried

Dijon dressing

60mls	(¹/₄ cup) extra virgin olive oil
¹/₂	lemon, juiced
1 tsp	Dijon mustard
	Salt & ground black pepper, to taste

1 Preheat oven to 180°C (350°F). Line a baking tray with non-stick baking paper and place the prosciutto on the lined tray. Cook prosciutto in preheated oven for 7 minutes or until crisp. Set aside.

2 Meanwhile, to make the dressing, place the olive oil, lemon juice and the mustard in a small bowl. Season with salt and pepper and whisk to combine.

3 Cook the snow peas in small saucepan of salted boiling water for 1 minute or until bright green. Drain and refresh in iced water. Drain. Halve the avocados, remove the seeds, peel and cut into large cubes.

4 Just before serving, break the prosciutto into small pieces and combine gently with the snow peas, avocados and radicchio in a serving bowl. Pour the dressing over and toss to combine.

BROCCOLI

■ Make a warm salad by boiling some broccoli florets until tender-crisp. Drain and toss while still warm with strips of roasted red capsicum (pepper), a little extra virgin olive oil, some garlic, capers and chopped fresh parsley. Season well and serve with fish or chicken.

■ For a simple accompaniment, plunge some broccoli florets into boiling water and cook for 3–4 minutes or until bright green. Drain and then toss with plenty of crushed garlic. Drizzle with a little olive oil and lemon juice while still warm. Serve warm or at room temperature. This dish is also good topped with pieces of crisp bacon.

■ Stir-fry broccoli florets in a little peanut oil with garlic, ginger and red chilli. Add some oyster sauce when tender and heat through. Serve immediately.

good broccoli partners: mint, pine nuts, soy sauce, cream, butter, olive oil, bacon, garlic, anchovies, lemon juice, cheese sauce, walnuts.

This dish doesn't quite have the same creamy texture of a traditional potato gratin where the potatoes are simply baked in cream and flavoured with a touch of garlic. It does, however, contain only about 2½ grams of fat per serve and the flavour is just as irresistible.

low-fat potato gratin

serves: 4 prep: 10 mins cooking: 1½ hours

	Extra light olive oil spray, for greasing
800g	**(1¾ pounds) potatoes (like nicola or desiree)**
100g	**(½ cup) low-fat natural yoghurt**
60g	**(¼ cup) sour light cream**
125mls	**(½ cup) low-fat milk**
1 tbs	**wholegrain mustard**
	Salt & ground black pepper, to taste
¼ tsp	**ground nutmeg**
2	**garlic cloves, very thinly sliced**

1 Preheat oven to 200°C (400°F). Spray a 1.5-litre (6-cup) rectangular ovenproof dish with the olive oil spray.

2 Peel and thinly slice the potatoes. Combine the yoghurt, sour cream, milk and mustard in a small bowl. Spoon 2 tbs of the yoghurt mixture over the bottom of the ovenproof dish.

3 Arrange one fifth of the sliced potatoes over the yoghurt. Season with a pinch of salt, pepper and nutmeg and top with another 2 tbs of the yoghurt mixture. Continue to layer the potatoes, salt, pepper, nutmeg, and yoghurt mixture, adding garlic slices from time to time to form 5 layers. Finish with a layer of the remaining yoghurt mixture.

4 Bake in preheated oven for 1½ hours or until the liquid is absorbed, potatoes are tender and the top is golden. Cover with foil if the potatoes begin to brown too quickly. Serve warm.

spinach pie

serves: 4   prep: 20 mins (plus 20 mins cooling time)   cooking: 55–65 mins

Extra light olive oil spray, to grease
2 large brown onions, finely chopped
2 garlic cloves, crushed
2 tbs fresh lemon juice
1 bunch silverbeet, washed, stalks trimmed and discarded, leaves shredded
2 eggs, lightly whisked
110g (¹/₂ cup) low-fat cottage cheese
70g (3 tbs) Greek feta, crumbled
¹/₂ cup chopped fresh continental parsley
1 tbs wholegrain mustard
2 tsp cracked black pepper
1 tsp ground nutmeg
Salt, to taste
5 sheets filo pastry
2 tsp poppy seeds

1 Preheat oven to 180°C (350°F). Lightly spray a 14 x 26cm or 5.5 x 10 in (base measurement) (1.5-litre/6-cup capacity) ovenproof dish with olive oil spray to grease.

2 Combine the onions, garlic and lemon juice in a large saucepan and cook over medium heat, stirring occasionally with a wooden spoon, for 5 minutes or until the onion starts to soften.

3 Add half the silverbeet to the pan, cover and cook, stirring occasionally, for 2–3 minutes or until just wilted. Remove from the pan and repeat with the remaining silverbeet. Return all the silverbeet to the saucepan and cook, uncovered, for a further 5–8 minutes, stirring occasionally, or until the liquid has evaporated. Transfer to a bowl and place in the fridge for 20 minutes or until cool.

4 Add the eggs, cottage cheese, feta, parsley, mustard, pepper and nutmeg to the silverbeet mixture and stir well to combine. Season with salt.

5 Lay the filo sheets on a work bench, cover with a clean tea towel and then a damp tea towel to prevent pastry from drying out. Working quickly, lay 3 sheets of filo over the ovenproof dish and gently mould the filo to the shape of the dish, allowing the edges to overlap the dish.

6 Spoon the silverbeet mixture evenly into the dish. Fold the remaining 2 sheets of filo in half and place over the top of the pie. Use wet fingertips to roll the edges of the pastry together to form an edge around the pie. Lightly spray the top of the pie with the olive oil spray. Sprinkle with the poppy seeds.

7 Bake in preheated oven for 45 minutes until the filling is firm and pastry is golden. Serve immediately.

Good mash with an irresistible creamy texture comes down to two things—the right potato variety and the right method. You need a potato that is 'floury' (see potato chart p 156). Boiling potatoes whole in their skin will stop them absorbing excess moisture. Another good tip is to use potatoes that are evenly sized so they take the same length of time to cook. Enjoy!

garlic mashed potato

serves: 6   prep: 15–20 mins   cooking: 30 mins

1kg (2.2 pounds) evenly-sized medium potatoes (like king edward)
Salt & ground black pepper, to taste
2 large garlic cloves, finely chopped
150mls (²/₃ cup) milk
125g (7 tbs) butter, diced, at room temperature

1 Carefully wash the unpeeled potatoes to remove any dirt without breaking their skins. Leave the potatoes whole. Place them in a large heavy-based saucepan, cover with cold water and add 1 tsp salt. Bring to the boil over high heat. Reduce heat to medium-high and gently boil, uncovered, for 30 minutes (depending on the size of the potatoes) or until soft. Test by piercing the potatoes right through the centre with a skewer towards the end of cooking. Don't pierce the potatoes too often during cooking or they will absorb excess water.

2 Drain the cooked potatoes in a colander and stand for about 5 minutes to allow them to cool slightly.

3 Meanwhile, place the milk and garlic in a small saucepan over low heat and bring just to a simmer. (See microwave tip.) Remove the milk from heat and keep warm.

4 Peel away the potato skins. Return the potatoes to the dry saucepan. Place the saucepan over medium-low heat and, if necessary, gently shake the pan for 30–60 seconds or until all the excess moisture evaporates.

5 Use a potato masher to mash the potatoes until they are partially mashed. (Never use a food processor or you will end up with glue.) Gradually add the butter and continue to mash until the potato is smooth.

6 Remove the garlic from the milk and discard. Add half the warmed milk to the potato mixture and use a wooden spoon to beat vigorously until the milk is incorporated and the mixture is smooth. Add the remaining milk and beat until light and fluffy. Season with salt and pepper and serve immediately.

microwave tip: place the milk and garlic in a microwave-safe jug or bowl and heat, uncovered, for 1–2 minute on Medium/500watts/50% or until just

These brownies will keep in an airtight container at room temperature for up to 5 days—if they're not devoured first. Try serving them warm with vanilla ice-cream.

chocolate &
hazelnut brownies

makes: about 20   prep: 15 mins   cooking: 45 mins

Melted butter, for greasing
200g   (1¹/₃ cups) hazelnuts
250g   (9 oz) good-quality dark chocolate, broken into pieces
175g   (9 tbs) butter, cubed
3   eggs
220g   (1 cup) caster sugar
1 tsp vanilla essence
150g   (1 cup) plain flour
¹/₂ tsp   baking powder
¹/₂ tsp   salt

1 Preheat oven to 160°C (325°F). Brush a 20 x 30cm (8 x 11 in) slab pan with the melted butter to grease and then line the base with non-stick baking paper.

2 Spread the hazelnuts over a baking tray and toast in preheated oven for 5 minutes or until aromatic. Transfer the hazelnuts onto a clean tea towel and rub with the tea towel to remove as much of the skins as possible. Discard the skins. Roughly chop the hazelnuts and set aside.

3 Place the chocolate and butter in a heat-resistant bowl and stir over a saucepan of simmering water until the mixture is melted and combined. Set aside.

4 Use electric beaters or a hand whisk to whisk the eggs and sugar in a medium mixing bowl until thick and creamy. Add the melted chocolate mixture and vanilla essence and whisk to combine.

5 Sift together flour, baking powder and salt. Use a large metal spoon to fold flour mixture and reserved hazelnuts gently through chocolate mixture.

6 Pour the mixture into the prepared pan and bake in preheated oven for 35–40 minutes or until crumbs cling to a skewer inserted into the centre.

7 Remove from the oven and cool in the pan. Turn onto a cutting board and cut into serving portions.

CHOCOLATE & COCOA POWDER

■ My granny's favourite chocolate sauce is made like this: stir 330g (1¹/₂ cups) sugar, 250mls (1 cup) water and 2 tbs golden syrup in a saucepan over medium heat until sugar dissolves. Bring to the boil. Combine 125g (1¹/₄ cups) cocoa powder and 1¹/₂ tbs cornflour in a bowl. Gradually mix in 125mls (¹/₂ cup) water to make a smooth paste. Add to sugar mixture with 1 tsp butter and ¹/₂ tsp vanilla essence and stir to combine. Bring back to the boil and simmer for a few minutes. Serve warm—it is especially good when poured generously over sponge cake and vanilla ice-cream.

■ Make a rich hot chocolate by combining 250mls (1 cup) milk with 80g (3 oz) chopped good quality milk or dark chocolate and ¹/₂ tsp vanilla essence. Stir over low heat until heated though.

good chocolate partners: caramel, strawberries, cream, coffee, vanilla ice-cream, dried figs, dark rum, brandy, pecans, prunes.

self-saucing chocolate pudding

serves: 4   prep: 10 mins   cooking: 20 mins

Melted butter or margarine,
for greasing
110g   (³/₄ cup) self-raising flour
3 tsp   cocoa powder
40g   (2 tbs) butter
50g   (¹/₃ cup, lightly packed)
        brown sugar
1   egg, lightly whisked
80mls   (¹/₃ cup) milk
        Thick (whipped) cream (optional),
        to serve

sauce
40g   (¹/₄ cup, lightly packed)
        brown sugar
2 tsp   cocoa powder, sifted
185mls (³/₄ cup) boiling water

1 Preheat oven to 180°C (350°F). Brush four 125mls (¹/₂-cup) ramekins or soufflé dishes with the melted butter or margarine to grease. Place on a baking tray lined with non-stick baking paper.

2 Sift together flour and cocoa powder into a small bowl. Use electric beaters to beat the butter and brown sugar in a medium mixing bowl until pale and creamy. Add the egg and beat until combined. Add the flour mixture and milk to the butter mixture and use a large metal spoon to fold until just combined. Spoon into the greased dishes.

3 For the sauce, combine the brown sugar and cocoa powder and sprinkle evenly over pudding mixture. Carefully pour the boiling water over the puddings, dividing evenly.

4 Bake in preheated oven for 20 minutes or until a skewer inserted into the top of the puddings comes out clean and a sauce forms underneath. Remove from the oven and stand for 3–4 minutes before serving.

carrot cake

makes: 18 slices   prep: 15 mins   cooking: 35 mins

	Vegetable oil, for greasing
150g	(1 cup) plain flour
120g	(³/₄ cup) wholemeal plain flour
2 tsp	bicarbonate of soda (baking soda)
1 tsp	baking powder
1 tsp	freshly grated or ground nutmeg
250g	(1¹/₄ cups, firmly packed) brown sugar
400g	(about 2 medium) carrots, peeled, coarsely grated
100g	(¹/₂ cup) walnuts, roughly chopped
3	eggs
250mls	(1 cup) vegetable oil

cream cheese icing

160g	(3 oz) cream cheese
75g	(¹/₂ cup) icing (powdered) sugar, sifted
1	orange, rind finely grated

1 Preheat oven to 180°C (350°F). Brush a square 20cm (8 in) cake pan with the vegetable oil to grease and then line the base with non-stick baking paper.

2 Sift together the plain flour, wholemeal flour, bicarbonate of soda, baking powder and nutmeg into a large bowl. Return bran to the flour. Add the brown sugar, grated carrot and walnuts and mix well.

3 Combine the eggs and vegetable oil in a medium mixing bowl and use a hand whisk to whisk until pale. Add to the dry ingredients and use a large metal spoon to fold until just combined.

4 Spoon the cake mixture into prepared pan and bake in preheated oven for 35 minutes or until a skewer inserted into the centre of the cake comes out clean. Stand in pan for 10 minutes before turning onto a wire rack to cool completely.

5 To make the icing, place the cream cheese, icing sugar and orange rind in the bowl of a food processor and process until smooth.

6 Spread the icing over the cooled cake and serve cut into slices. Keep in an airtight container in the fridge for up to 3 days.

Juicy tangelos are a cross between a mandarin and a grapefruit which is reflected in their sweet but tangy flavour. They are a good substitute for oranges and will impart a more intense flavour when used. Here they are teamed with mandarins and spiced with cardamom for an extremely quick dessert.

warm citrus fruit in cardamom cream

serves: 4 prep: 5–10 mins cooking: 4–6 mins

20g	(1 tbs) butter
2 tbs	brown sugar
$^1/_2$ tsp	ground cardamom
80mls	($^1/_3$ cup) thickened cream
3	tangelos, peeled, segmented
2	mandarins, peeled, segmented
	Thickened (whipped) cream or vanilla ice-cream, to serve

1 Melt the butter in a medium frying pan over medium-low heat. Add the brown sugar and cardamom and stir constantly for 1–2 minutes or until the sugar dissolves.

2 Stir in the cream. Add the tangelo and mandarin segments and cook, stirring constantly, for 1–2 minutes or until the segments are just warm. (See microwave tip.)

3 Serve warm with cream or ice-cream.

microwave tip: place the butter, brown sugar and cardamom in a medium heat-resistant microwave-safe dish. Heat, uncovered, for 2 minutes on Medium-High/650watts/70% or until sugar dissolves. Stir in the cream until well combined. Add the tangelo and mandarin segments and heat for 1–2 minutes on Medium/500watts/50% or until segments are just warm.

This birthday cake is a simple butter cake decorated with icing sugar and hundreds and thousands or sprinkles. You can make it using a stencil made from the star template in the index.

star birthday cake

serves: 12   prep: 20 mins   cooking: 1 hour 25 mins

Melted butter or margarine, for greasing

200g (1¹/₂ cup) butter, at room temperature

330g (1¹/₂ cups) caster sugar

1 tsp vanilla essence

4 eggs

450g (3 cups) self-raising flour

Pinch of salt

175mls (³/₄ cup) milk

Icing (powdered) sugar, to decorate

Hundreds and thousands (sprinkles), to decorate

Birthday cake candles, to decorate

1 Preheat oven to 160°C (325°F). Brush a deep, round 22cm (8.5 in) cake pan with the melted butter or margarine to lightly grease and then line the base with non-stick baking paper.

2 Use electric beaters to beat the butter, sugar and vanilla essence in a large mixing bowl until pale and creamy. Add the eggs one at a time, and beat well after each addition.

3 Sift together the self-raising flour and salt. On the lowest speed, mix the sifted flour into the butter mixture alternately with the milk in three separate batches of each. Be careful not to overmix.

4 Spoon the cake mixture into the prepared cake pan and bake in preheated oven for 1 hour and 25 minutes or until cooked through and a skewer inserted into the centre comes out clean. Remove from oven and stand in the cake pan for 5 minutes before turning onto a wire rack to cool completely.

5 To decorate, use the star shape in the index as a guide and cut out a template with a star-shaped hole. Trim the top of the cake to form a level surface and turn the cake upside down onto a serving plate making the bottom the top. Sprinkle the surface liberally with icing sugar. Carefully place the star-shape template on the cake and sprinkle with hundreds and thousands to form a star on the surface. Decorate with the appropriate number of candles.

Rhubarb is a vegetable but it is best used as a fruit and cooked with sugar to sweeten the tart, rosy-coloured stalks. It is important to remember that the green rhubarb leaves are poisonous so make sure you discard them.

rhubarb with orange & honey

serves: 4 prep: 25 mins (plus 15 mins chilling time) cooking: 10 mins

1   bunch rhubarb
1   orange
2 tbs   honey
2 tbs   water
2   200g (7 oz) cartons vanilla Frûche

1 Cut the leaves from rhubarb and discard. Wash the stalks and cut into 2cm lengths. Finely grate the rind from the orange and then juice the fruit.

2 Combine the rhubarb pieces, 1 tsp orange rind, 60mls ($^1/_4$ cup) orange juice, honey and water in a medium saucepan. Bring to a simmer over medium-low heat. Cover and cook for 5–8 minutes, stirring occasionally, or until the rhubarb is tender but still holding its shape. (See microwave tip.)

3 Transfer the rhubarb to a bowl and place it in the freezer for 15 minutes, stirring occasionally, or until cool.

4 Layer the rhubarb and vanilla Frûche in individual dishes. Serve immediately.

microwave tip: combine the rhubarb pieces, 1 tsp orange rind, 60mls ($^1/_4$ cup) orange juice, honey and water in a medium heat-resistant microwave-safe bowl. Cover and cook for 2–4 minutes on High/850watts/100% or until just tender but still holding its shape.

pan-fried pears with maple syrup orange & pecans

serves: 4 prep: 10 mins cooking: 10 mins

40g (2 tbs) butter
2 ripe (about 300g) pears (like beurre bosc, packham or williams), peeled, cut into very thin slices
2 tbs maple syrup
1/2 tsp finely grated orange rind
80mls (1/3 cup) fresh orange juice
40g (1/3 cup) chopped pecan nuts
Vanilla ice-cream, to serve

1 Melt half the butter in a large frying pan over medium-high heat. Add half the pear slices and cook for 2 minutes or until golden underneath. Turn the slices and cook for a further 2 minutes, or until just tender. Remove the pears with a slotted spoon and place into a shallow serving dish. Add the remaining pears to the pan and repeat the cooking process.

2 Return the frying pan to medium-high heat. Add the remaining butter, maple syrup, orange rind and juice and pecans. Bring to the boil, stirring constantly. Pour the hot sauce over the pears and serve over the ice-cream.

MANDARINS

■ To make a dressing to toss through finely sliced carrot and fennel, combine 3 tbs mandarin juice with 3 tbs sour cream, 1 tsp grated fresh ginger and 1 1/2 tsp poppy seeds.

■ Peel about 8 mandarins. Slice or divide them into segments and then layer with some torn fresh mint leaves. Stir 150g (2/3 cup) sugar and 250mls (1 cup) water in a small saucepan over medium heat until sugar dissolves. Bring to the boil and simmer for 10 minutes. Pour over mandarins and serve warm or at room temperature with cream or natural yoghurt.

■ Combine mandarin segments and wedges of cooked fresh beetroot with a dressing of mandarin juice, wholegrain mustard, honey and olive oil for a fantastic salad to serve with chargrilled chicken or pork.

good mandarin partners: honey, cardamom, cinnamon, mint, beetroot, cream, sour cream, carrots, beetroot, beans.

Friands – small, rich almond cakes – have become enormously popular in recent times with many cafes serving them. They are surprisingly quick and simple to make and they keep very well in an airtight container for up to 2 days. Individual, oval-shaped friand pans are available from good kitchenware shops but you can use 80ml (1/3 cup) muffin pans if you like.

orange & poppy seed friands

makes: 10   prep: 15 mins (plus 5 mins standing time)   cooking: 20–25 mins

	Melted butter, for greasing
75g	(1/2 cup) plain flour
190g	(11/4 cups) icing sugar mixture
150g	(11/2 cups) almond meal
2 tbs	poppy seeds
1	large orange, rind finely grated
5	egg whites
180g	(9 tbs) butter, melted, cooled
90g	(1/4 cup) orange marmalade

1 Preheat oven to 200°C (400°F). Brush 10 friand pans with the melted butter, to grease, and place on a baking tray.

2 Sift the flour and icing sugar into a large mixing bowl. Stir in the almond meal, poppy seeds and orange rind.

3 Use electric beaters or a hand whisk to lightly whisk the egg whites in a large mixing bowl until frothy but not firm. Use a large metal spoon to fold the egg whites into the dry ingredients. Add the melted butter and stir until just combined. Spoon the mixture into the prepared pans to fill three quarters full.

4 Bake in preheated oven for 20–25 minutes or until golden and a skewer inserted in the centre comes out clean. Stand the friands in the pans for 5 minutes before turning onto a wire rack.

5 Place the marmalade in a small saucepan and gently warm over low heat, stirring occasionally, until melted. Brush the tops of the warm friands with the warm marmalade and allow to cool.

Crème brûlée without the brûlée! These little custard desserts can be made up to 2 days ahead of serving and kept covered with plastic wrap in the fridge. Likewise, the sweet oranges can be made up to 4 days ahead and kept in an airtight container in the fridge.

luscious custard pots
with sweet oranges

serves: 8   prep: 25 mins (plus 1 hour cooling time)   cooking: 1 hour

500mls	(2 cups) thin cream
300mls	(1¹/₄ cups) milk
8	egg yolks
75g	(¹/₃ cup) caster sugar
¹/₄ tsp	ground cinnamon
1 tsp	vanilla essence
	Almond bread, to serve

sweet oranges

4	oranges
440g	(2 cups) sugar
250mls	(1 cup) water

1 Preheat oven to 180°C (350°F).

2 Combine the cream and milk in a medium saucepan and heat over medium-low heat, stirring occasionally, until just simmering. Remove from heat and set aside for 5 minutes to cool slightly.

3 Meanwhile, place egg yolks, caster sugar, cinnamon and vanilla essence in a medium mixing bowl and use electric beaters to beat until thick and creamy. Add the cream mixture and stir to combine.

4 Pour the custard mixture into eight 125mls (¹/₂-cup) ramekins. Place the ramekins in a baking dish and add enough hot tap water to the dish to reach halfway up the sides of the ramekins. Bake in preheated oven for 25 minutes or until just set.

5 Remove the ramekins immediately from the baking dish and place in the fridge to cool.

6 Meanwhile, to make the sweet oranges, juice 1 orange and reserve the juice. Peel the rind from the 3 remaining oranges using a vegetable peeler. Remove the white pith from the rind and cut the rind into thin strips and reserve. (Alternatively use a zester.) Remove all the white pith from the oranges and cut the oranges into 1cm-thick slices. Place the orange flesh in a bowl and set aside until needed.

7 Combine reserved orange juice, sugar and water in a medium saucepan and stir over medium-high heat until sugar dissolves. Bring to the boil, reduce heat to low and add the reserved orange rind strips. Simmer gently, uncovered, for 30 minutes or until the syrup is thick and the orange rind is translucent. Remove from the heat, add the reserved orange slices and set aside to cool for about 1 hour.

8 One hour before serving, remove the custard pots from the fridge and bring to room temperature. Place the orange slices on top of the custard pots. Spoon over some of the syrup and decorate with the orange rind. Serve accompanied by the almond bread.

vegetarian autumn lunch for 4

vegetable tagine with yellow split peas (p 121)

crusty bread

lemon & lime tart (p 139)

casual spring lunch for 6

Mediterranean lamb burgers on Turkish bread (p 27)

chocolate cake (p 50) served with thick cream or ice-cream and seasonal berries

long winter lunch for 8

garlic & potato pizza x 2 (p 158)

braised chicken with tomato, capers & olives (p 172)

cumin-roasted potatoes (p 172)

winter salad (p 178)

orange & poppy seed friands (p 194)

quick summer weekday dinner for 4

seared fish salad (p 76)

strawberries with orange syrup & ice-cream (p 93)

light spring dinner for 6

vegetable lasagne (p 21)

pineapple & mint granita (p 53)

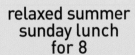

quick winter
meal for 4

prawn & noodle soup
with coriander paste (p 163)

pan-fried pears with
maple syrup, orange
& pecans (p 193)

relaxed summer
sunday lunch
for 8

fresh oysters with mango
& red capsicum salsa (p 60)

orange & oregano lamb with
barbecued vegetables (p 71)

tossed green salad

peaches basted with honey
& wine (p 95) or
fresh fruit pops (p 86)

autumn sunday brunch for 8

fresh date & bran loaf with vanilla yoghurt spread (p 149)

banana & pecan muffins (p 136)

grilled mushrooms (p 127)

seasonal fruit

freshly squeezed orange juice

storage
making fruit, vegetables & herbs last

■ **apples** in the crisper section or in a sealed plastic bag in the fridge. They will lose their crispness 10 times faster if stored at room temperature. Keep in the fridge for up to 4 weeks. Their texture will become more grainy over time.

■ **apricots** ripen at room temperature out of direct sunlight. When ripe the fruit will yield to gentle pressure, have no signs of green and have a sweet apricot aroma. Once ripe, keep in a sealed plastic bag or airtight container in the fridge and use within 2 days.

■ **artichokes**
globe artichokes in a sealed plastic bag in the fridge for up to 3 days.
Jerusalem artichokes unwashed in an unsealed plastic bag in the crisper section of the fridge for up to 2 weeks.

■ **Asian greens** in a sealed plastic bag in the fridge or in an unsealed plastic bag in the crisper section for up to 3 days.

■ **asparagus** stand the spears upright in a glass containing 1-2 cm of water and cover with a plastic bag. Keep in the fridge for 2-3 days.

■ **avocados** in a cool, well-ventilated place out of direct sunlight until ripe (usually 3-5 days). To hasten ripening place in a paper bag with a ripe banana at room temperature. The fruit will yield to gentle pressure at the stem end when ripe. Avocados will start deteriorating once ripe and are best eaten as soon as possible. However, if you need to store them once ripe they will keep in the fridge for up to 3 days.

■ **bananas** ripen at room temperature out of direct sunlight. To hasten ripening place the unripe banana in a paper bag with a ripe banana. To extend their life, wrap ripe bananas in several layers of newspaper and place in the fridge for up to 3 days. The skins will turn black but the flesh inside will be fine.

■ **beans** in a sealed plastic bag in the fridge or in an unsealed plastic bag in the crisper section for up to 3 days.

■ **beetroot (beets)** cut the leaves from the bulbs leaving at least 5cm of the stalks attached to the bulbs. Store the leaves and the bulbs in separate sealed plastic bags in the fridge. Use the leaves within 2 days. The bulbs will last for up to 2 weeks.

■ **berries** use as soon as possible. If you need to store them spread on a plate lined with paper towel, cover with plastic wrap and keep in the fridge.

■ **broccoli** will keep in a sealed plastic bag in the fridge or in an unsealed plastic bag in crisper for up to 3 days.

■ **brussels sprouts** in a sealed plastic bag in the fridge or in an unsealed plastic bag in crisper for up to 3 days.

■ **cabbage** store whole cabbages in a cool, well-ventilated place for up to 2 weeks. Wrap cut cabbage in plastic wrap and store in the crisper section of the fridge for up to 2 days.

■ **capsicum (pepper)** in the crisper section or in a sealed plastic bag in the fridge for up to 1 week.

■ **carambola (star fruit)** ripen at room temperature. The fruit will turn a golden yellow colour and the edge of the ribs will become brown when ripe. Once ripe, keep in a sealed plastic bag in the fridge or in an unsealed plastic bag in the crisper for up to 3 days.

■ **carrots** in a sealed plastic bag in the crisper section of the fridge for up to 1 week.

■ **cauliflower** remove all but the inner leaves and keep in a sealed plastic bag in the fridge or in an unsealed plastic bag in the crisper section for up to 3 days.

■ **celeriac (celery root)** remove the tops and place in a sealed plastic bag in the fridge for up to 5 days.

■ **celery** in a sealed plastic bag in the fridge for up to 3 days.

■ **cherries** in a sealed plastic bag in the fridge. Use as soon as possible.

■ **chestnuts** in an airtight container or paper bag in the fridge for up to 3 weeks.

■ **chillies** in the crisper section or in a sealed plastic bag in the fridge for up to 1 week.

■ **corn** still wrapped in its husk in a sealed plastic bag in the fridge.

■ **cucumbers** in the crisper section of the fridge.

■ **cumquats** in a cool, well-ventilated place for up to 5 days or in a sealed plastic bag in the fridge for 2 weeks.

■ **custard apple** ripen at room temperature out of direct sunlight for 3-5 days. The fruit will yield to gentle pressure when ripe. Once ripe, keep in the fridge and use within 2 days.

■ **dates** in a sealed plastic bag or airtight container in the fridge for at least 1 month or in the freezer for at least 6 months.

■ **eggplant** in the crisper section of the fridge for up to 1 week.

■ **fennel** in a sealed plastic bag in the crisper section for up to 1 week.

■ **figs** in a single layer on a plate lined with paper towel in the fridge for up to 3 days.

■ **garlic** in a cool, dry, dark well-ventilated place (try a garlic basket or bag) for at least 1 month.

■ **ginger** wrap in foil and keep in the crisper section of the fridge for up to 2 weeks. It will keep indefinitely if peeled and kept in a sealed freezer bag or airtight container in the freezer. Grate off the required amount and return remaining ginger to the freezer. Alternatively, place peeled in a glass jar, cover with sherry or gin and keep in the fridge indefinitely.

■ **grapefruit** in a cool, well-ventilated place out of direct sunlight for up to 2 weeks. In warmer weather keep it in the crisper (vegetable) section of the fridge for up to 1 month.

■ **grapes** unwashed in a sealed air-tight container or plastic bag in the fridge. Use them as soon as possible or at least within 3 days.

■ **guava** ripen at room temperature out of direct sunlight until ripe. The fruit will yield to gentle pressure when ripe. Once ripe, place in a sealed plastic bag in the fridge or in the crisper section. Use within 3 days.

■ **honeydew melon** store whole at room temperature out of direct sunlight and use within 2-3 days. Once cut, cover with plastic wrap and store in the fridge. Use as soon as possible.

■ **kohlrabi** remove and discard the leaves. Store the bulbs in a sealed plastic bag in the fridge or in an unsealed plastic bag in the crisper (vegetable) section for up to 4 days.

■ **leeks** trim and discard the tops. Keep in a sealed plastic bag in the crisper section for up to 1 week.

■ **lemons** in a cool, well-ventilated place out of direct sunlight for at least 1 week. Or in the crisper section of the fridge for at least 3 weeks.

■ **lettuce** place, unwashed, in a lettuce keeper, airtight container or sealed plastic bag in the fridge for up to 5 days.

■ **limes** at room temperature out of direct sunlight for up to 2 weeks. Or, keep in a sealed plastic bag in the fridge or an unsealed plastic bag in the crisper section for up to 1 month.

■ **loquat (rush orange)** at room temperature out of direct sunlight for up to 3 days. Or, in a sealed plastic bag in the fridge for up to 5 days.

■ **lychees** in a sealed plastic bag in the fridge for up to 1 week.

■ **mandarins** in a cool, well-ventilated place out of direct sunlight for up

to 5 days. Or in a sealed plastic bag in the fridge or unsealed plastic bag in the crisper section for up to 2 weeks.

■ **mangoes** at room temperature for 2-3 days or until ripe. When ripe the fruit will yield to gentle pressure when cradled in your hand and will have a strong, sweet aroma. Once ripe eat as soon as possible.

■ **mushrooms** in a paper or cloth bag (to prevent sweating) in the fridge.

■ **nashi** in the crisper section or in a sealed plastic bag in the fridge for up to 2 weeks.

■ **nectarines** ripen at room temperature out of direct sunlight. The fruit will yield to gentle pressure at the stem end when ripe. Once ripe, place them in the crisper section or in a sealed plastic bag in the fridge and use within 3 days.

■ **okra** in an unsealed plastic bag in the crisper section of the fridge for up to 5 days.

■ **onions**

brown, red/Spanish, white, French shallots/eschallots in a dry, cool, dark, well-ventilated place for up to 1 month.

green onions/green shallots/scallions wrap in paper towel and place in a sealed plastic bag in the crisper section of the fridge for up to 7 days.

spring onions trim the tops and place in a sealed plastic bag in the crisper section of the fridge for up to 7 days.

■ **oranges** in a cool, well-ventilated place out of direct sunlight for up to 2 weeks. Or, in a sealed plastic bag in the fridge for up to 1 month.

■ **papaya** ripen at room temperature. The fruit will yield to gentle pressure at the stem end (slightly more than a ripe avocado) when ripe. Once ripe, store in the fridge for up to 4 days. Once cut, cover cut surface with plastic wrap and store in the fridge for up to 2 days.

■ **parsnip** in an unsealed plastic bag in the crisper section of the fridge for up to 1 week.

■ **passionfruit** at room temperature out of direct sunlight for up to 1 week. Or, keep in the crisper section of the fridge for at least 2 weeks.

■ **pawpaw** ripen at room temperature. The fruit will yield to gentle pressure when ripe. Once ripe, store in the

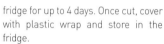

fridge for up to 4 days. Once cut, cover with plastic wrap and store in the fridge.

■ **peaches** ripen at room temperature out of direct sunlight. The fruit will have a rich yellow colour at the stem end when ripe. Once ripe store in a unsealed plastic bag in the fridge and use within 3 days.

■ **pears** ripen at room temperature out of direct sunlight. The fruit will yield to medium pressure at the stem end when ripe. Once ripe place in an open plastic bag or paper bag in the fridge and use within 3 days.

■ **peas (green)** in a sealed plastic bag in the fridge for up to 5 days. (See p 203 for snow and sugar snap peas).

■ **persimmons** ripen at room temperature out of direct sunlight. The fruit will yield to gentle pressure when ripe. Once ripe use as soon as possible or place in a sealed plastic bag in the fridge for up to 2 days.

■ **pineapple** use as soon as possible. Keep whole pineapple at room temperature out of direct sunlight for up to 4 days. Once cut cover with plastic wrap and keep in the fridge for up to 3 days. It will keep for the same length of time if peeled and placed in a sealed airtight container in the fridge.

■ **plums** ripen at room temperature

out of direct sunlight. The fruit will yield to gentle pressure when ripe. Once ripe store in an unsealed plastic bag in the fridge for up to 2 weeks.

■ **pomegranates** at room temperature out of direct sunlight for up to 5 days. Or keep in a sealed plastic bag in the fridge for up to 2 weeks.

■ **pomelos** store in a cool, well-ventilated place out of direct sunlight for up to 2 weeks. Or store in a sealed plastic bag in the fridge for up to 1 month.

■ **potatoes** in a cool, dry, dark, well-ventilated place for up to 2 weeks. Never store in a plastic bag as they will sweat or in the fridge.

■ **pumpkin** store whole pumpkins in a cool, dry, well-ventilated place for up to 2-3 months. Once cut, remove the seeds, wrap in plastic wrap or place in a sealed plastic bag and keep in the fridge for up to 3 days.

■ **quince** store in a single layer in a cool, dry place out of direct sunlight for up to 2 weeks. Or keep in a sealed plastic bag in the fridge for up to 1 month.

■ **radish** remove the leaves from the bulbs. Store young tender leaves in a sealed plastic bag in the fridge for up to 3 days. Store bulbs in a sealed plastic bag in the fridge for up to 1 week.

- **rambutans** at room temperature for up to 4 days or in a sealed plastic bag in the crisper section of the fridge for up to 10 days.
- **rockmelon (cantaloupe)** store whole in a cool, well-ventilated place out of direct sunlight for up to 5 days. Once cut, cover with plastic wrap and keep in the fridge for up to 3 days.
- **rhubarb** cut away the leaves and discard. Store stalks in a sealed plastic bag in the fridge for up to 1 week.
- **salad leaves** rinse leaves and dry. Wrap in paper towel or a clean tea towel and place in a sealed plastic bag in the crisper section of the fridge for up to 5 days.
- **silverbeet** trim stems and keep the leaves, unwashed, in a sealed plastic bag in the fridge for up to 3 days.
- **snow peas** in a sealed plastic bag in the fridge for up to 4 days.
- **spinach** keep bunches, unwashed, in a sealed plastic bag in the fridge for up to 4 days. Keep loose baby spinach the same way for up to 2 days.
- **squash** in a sealed plastic bag in the fridge for up to 3 days.
- **sugar snap peas** in a sealed plastic bag in the fridge or in an unsealed plastic bag in the crisper section for up to 4 days.
- **swede** in the crisper section of the fridge for up to 3 weeks.
- **sweet potato** in a cool, dry, dark, well-ventilated place for up to 1 week. Do not store in the fridge.
- **tamarillos** ripen at room temperature out of direct sunlight. The fruit will yield to gentle pressure when ripe. Once ripe, use as soon as possible.
- **tangelo** in a cool, well ventilated place out of direct sunlight for up to 2 weeks. Or, in an unsealed plastic bag in the fridge for at least 4 weeks.
- **tomatoes** ripen at room temperature out of direct sunlight. They are best used as soon as they ripen. Ripe tomatoes can be put in the fridge for up to 2 days. Bring them back to room temperature before using.
- **turnips** remove the leaves. Place the leaves in a sealed plastic bag and keep in the crisper section for up to 1 day. Store the bulbs the same way for up to 1 week.

- **watercress** wrap in damp paper towel and place in a sealed plastic bag in the crisper section of the fridge for up to 3 days.
- **watermelon** store whole in a cool, well-ventilated place out of direct sunlight for up to 2 weeks. Once cut, cover with plastic wrap and store in the fridge for up to 3 days.
- **witlof (chicory)** place in a brown paper bag or wrap in purple tissue paper to prevent it from turning green and bitter. Keep in the crisper section of the fridge for up to 2 days.
- **zucchini** in a sealed plastic bag in the fridge or in an unsealed plastic bag in the crisper section for up to 3 days.

herbs

basil wrap in paper towel or tea towel and place in a sealed plastic bag or airtight container in the fridge for up to 3 days.

chervil wrap in damp paper towel or tea towel and place in a plastic bag or airtight container in the fridge for up to 1 week.

chives wrap in damp paper towel or tea towel and place in a sealed plastic bag or airtight container in the fridge for up to 2 days.

coriander stand upright in a glass containing 1-2 cm water, cover loosely with a plastic bag and secure with an elastic band. Keep in the fridge for up to 5 days. Alternatively, wrap in damp paper towel or tea towel and place in a sealed plastic bag or airtight container in fridge.

dill wrap in damp paper towel or tea towel and place in a sealed plastic bag or airtight container in the fridge for up to 1 week.

marjoram wrap in damp paper towel or tea towel and place in a sealed plastic bag or airtight container in the fridge for up to 4 days.

mint wrap in damp paper towel or tea towel and place in a sealed plastic bag or airtight container in the fridge for up to 3 days.

oregano wrap in damp paper towel or tea towel and place in a sealed plastic bag or airtight container in the fridge for up to 5 days.

parsley stand upright in a glass containing 1-2 cm water, cover

loosely with a plastic bag and secure with an elastic band. Keep in the fridge for up to 5 days. Alternatively, wrap in damp paper towel or a tea towel and place in a sealed plastic bag or airtight container in the fridge for at least 1 week.

sage in a sealed plastic bag or airtight container in the fridge for up to 3 days.

rocket (arugula) wrap in damp paper towel or tea towel and place in a sealed plastic bag or airtight container in the fridge for up to 5 days.

rosemary in a sealed plastic bag or airtight container in the fridge for up to 1 week.

tarragon wrap in damp paper towel or clean tea towel and place in a sealed plastic bag or airtight container in the fridge for up to 1 week.

thyme wrap in damp paper towel or clean tea towel and place in a sealed plastic bag or airtight container in the fridge for up to 1 week.

Note:

crisper = vegetable section in the refrigerator.

..

index

trace this for star birthday cake page 190

acknowledgments

Many thanks to my husband Paul for his unfailing support. ƒ Lou Fay for her wonderful design. ƒ Janelle Bloom for her microwave tips and recipes. ƒ Sue Dodd, Sydney Markets Limited, for sharing her invaluable knowledge and time in helping compile the seasonal produce lists. ƒ Graham Liney, Australian Potato Seed Management, for his inexhaustible knowledge of potatoes and the wonderful potato cooking guide on p 156. ƒ Also, Text's Michael Heyward, Patty Brown, Lisa Green, Chong, Leanne George, Alison Turner, Jan Castorina and Joanne Hood for their practical help and advice. ƒ Christine Simpson, Fresh Finesse, Ian Manning, Perth Market Authority, Judy Bickmore, Adelaide Produce Markets, Bill Bishop, South Australian Farmers Federation, and Abigail Ulgiati, Queensland Fruit & Vegetable Growers for contributing to the seasonal produce lists. ƒ Also, Maria Papadopoulos, Sydney Fish Market, Jan Last, Rosemary Hemphill and Paul Urquhart. ƒ Annette Moore, Woodbyne Guesthouse, Jaspers Brush, NSW for the location for the spring chapter opener. ƒ Brett & Kate Guthrey, Kathleen Haven Orchard, Cobbitty, NSW for the location for summer chapter opener. ƒ Sydney Markets Limited, Flemington, NSW for the location for the autumn chapter opener. ƒ The All Seasons On Crown, Surry Hills, NSW for the kitchen location for the winter chapter opener. ƒ Jo Vella, Vella's Hydro Fresh for supplying lettuces for photography.

photographs:

quentin bacon 46, 48, 146
jon bader 142
adam bruzzone 147
verity chambers 75
chris chen 52
mark chew 69, 74, 80, 95, 122, 123
andrew elton 87, 93 (recipe)
rowan fotheringham 20, 165
andrew lehmann 42
louise lister 17, 39, 66, 81, 94, 98, 109, 112, 116, 132, 138, 168, 177, 192
mark o'meara 2, 6, 7, 8, 9, 10-11, 19, 21, 22, 25, 26, 28, 29, 34, 41, 43, 44, 53, 54-55, 61, 63, 64, 65, 68, 73, 77, 78, 84, 86, 90, 93 (berries), 97, 100-101, 107, 115, 119, 121, 125, 127, 129, 130, 134, 135, 137, 143, 148, 151, 152-153, 166, 167, 175, 178, 180, 182, 183, 186, 187, 189, 191, 200, 201, 202, 203, 208
ashley mackevicius 30, 32, 33, 36, 37, 120, 126, 170, 174
william meppem 18, 40, 70, 83, 88, 133, 160, 161, 173, 179, 190, 193, 196
john paul urizar 3, 47, 49, 51, 62, 92, 111, 141, 145, 159, 162, 163, 184, 185, 195

recipes:

kristen anderson 47, 63, 92, 184
janene brooks 24
kirsty cassidy 16. 19, 41, 43, 46, 53, 60, 67, 71, 79, 82, 89, 100, 113, 149, 158, 160, 161, 169, 199, 197

michele curtis 37, 94, 99, 120, 127, 171, 174
annette forrest 28, 64, 65, 76, 96, 124, 128, 134, 166, 188, 191
yael grinham 172, 178
fiona hammond 68, 75, 80, 95, 122, 123
jane hann 194
bettina jenkins 38, 81, 108, 117, 193
vicki liley 86
anneka manning 23, 27, 31, 32, 35, 36, 45, 49, 72, 91, 93, 118, 121, 131, 136, 140, 143, 144, 147, 187
lyndey milan 20, 33, 150, 164, 175, 183
suzie smith 40, 133, 139, 176
dimitra stais 50, 163
darienne sutton 21, 85, 106, 181, 182
alison turner 114, 186

styling:

kristen anderson 39, 47, 62, 81, 92, 109, 116, 185, 192
kirsty cassidy 3, 10-11, 17, 18, 20, 21, 30, 36, 42, 46, 52, 54-55, 66, 70, 83, 84, 88, 100-101, 107, 111, 112, 115, 152-153, 159, 160, 161, 165, 168, 180, 182, 186, 190, 196
marie-helen clauzon 51, 162
karen cotton 93 (recipe)
annette forrest 64, 97, 125, 129, 135, 167, 189, 191
yael grinham 2, 22, 25, 26, 29, 34, 41, 44, 61, 65, 73, 77, 78, 90, 119,

130, 137, 148, 151, 173, 175, 179, 183, 200-203
anneka manning 32, 48, 121, 141, 142, 145, 146, 187
fiona hammond 69, 74, 80, 95, 122, 123
jane hann 195
vicki liley 87
suzie smith 33, 37, 40, 94, 98, 120, 126, 132, 138, 170, 174, 177

stockists:

Thanks to the following stockists for generously supplying the props for photography:

Accoutrement, (02) 9969 1031
Alan Tillsley Antiques, (02) 9555 8782
Anibou, (02) 9319 0655
Bed, Bath N' Table Homewares, (03) 9387 3322
Burlington Centre Supermarket, (02) 9281 2777
Carmague, (02) 9960 6234
Chee Soo & Fitzgerald, (02) 9360 1031
Chefs' Warehouse, (02) 9211 4555
Cloth, (02) 9310 5095
Country Road Homewear, (03) 9267 1400
Dinosaur Designs (02) 9211 5353
Freedom Furniture, (02) 9951 9000
Funkis Swedish Forms, (02) 9130 6445

Home & Garden on the Mall, (02) 9235 1595
Hospitality Dinnerware, (03) 9529 3311
Hugh Webb Antiques, (02) 9331 5335
Ikea, (02) 9418 2744
Inne, (02) 9362 9900
Kangaroo Tent City, (02) 9519 1011
Kent Paper & Packaging Co., (02) 9949 6666
Le Creuset, 1800 811 119
Made In Japan, (02) 9360 6979
Major & Tom, (02) 9693 2404
Market Import, (03) 9500 0764
Michael A. Greene Antiques, (02) 9328 1712
No Chintz, (02) 9318 2080; (02) 9958 0257
Original Finish, (02) 9550 2365
Orson & Blake, (02) 9326 115
Papaya, (02) 9362 1620
Piggot's Store, (02) 9362 8119
Pillivuyt, (02) 9938 2400
Plane Tree Farm, (02) 9328 1276; (03) 9826 2466; (08) 9382 1075
Rice, (02) 9699 4083
Ruby Star Traders, (02) 9518 7899
Sanders & King, (03) 9500 1150
Shack, (02) 9960 5718
Supply & Demand, (03) 9428 6912
The Bay Tree, (02) 9328 1101
The Essential Ingredient, (02) 9550 5477
White, (02) 9968 4559